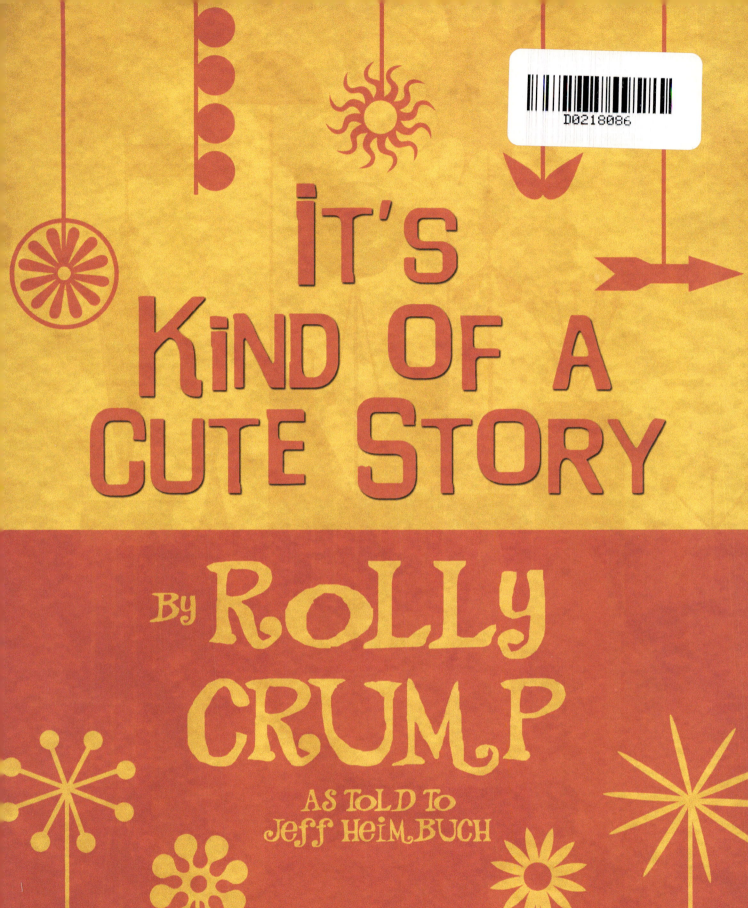

It's Kind Of A Cute Story

By Rolly Crump

As Told To Jeff Heimbuch

D0218086

Copyright 2012, Rolly Crump and Jeff Heimbuch
Cover Design: Pentakis Dodecahedron
Cover Painting: Rolly Crump
Interior Layout: Amy Inouye, Future Studio LA
Editor/Fact Checker: Hugh Allison

All Rights Reserved.

No part of this book may be reproduced in any form or by any electronic or mechanical means including information storage and retrieval systems, without permission in writing from the author. The only exception is by a reviewer, who may quote short excerpts in a review. This book is neither authorized nor sponsored nor endorsed by the Disney Company or any of its subsidiaries. It is an unofficial and unauthorized book and not a Disney product. The mention of names and places associated with the Disney Company and its businesses are not intended in any way to infringe on any existing copyrights or registered trademarks of the Disney Company but are used in context for educational purposes. The opinions and statements expressed in the quotations and text are solely the opinions of the author or those people who are quoted and do not necessarily reflect the opinions and policy of the Disney Company and its businesses nor Bamboo Forest Publishing. Although the Publishers and the Author of this book have made every effort to ensure the information was correct at the time of going to press, the Publishers and the Author do not assume and hereby disclaim any liability to any party for any loss or damage caused by errors, omissions, misleading information, or any potential travel disruption due to labor or financial difficulty, whether such errors or omissions result from negligence, accident, or any other cause.

All Photos Courtesy of Rolly Crump and Jeff Heimbuch, except for:

Photos Courtesy of Ken Kebow, pgs 12, 38, 48, 74, 82
Photo Courtesy of Kevin Kidney, pg 63
Photos Courtesy of Richard Harris, pgs 67, 68, 71, 73, 114, 117, 120, 121
Photos Courtesy of Jeff Lange, pgs 108-109
Photo Courtesy of Pentakis Dodecahedron, pg 129

ISBN: 978-0-9854706-4-7

Published by Bamboo Forest Publishing
First Printing: November, 2012

Visit us Online at:
www.bambooforestpublishing.com

PRAISE FOR IT'S KIND OF A CUTE STORY

"The most inspired, and inspiring, artist I've ever worked with was Rolly Crump. Period. I've always wondered how someone could have so much experience, and still retain a genuine sense of wonder and playfulness. Well, here's his story, and I loved every word of it. Lots of people talk about Walt Disney, but Rolly Crump can demonstrate the meaning of Walt Disney."

JIM STEINMEYER
former Imagineer

"Everyone who knew Walt Disney knew him differently, and that is why I love to read the stories of people like Rolly Crump. Rolly was never a yes man to Walt, and Walt obviously admired him for that. It is amazing to read his memoirs and realize how many of the major parts of the Disney parks were the work of this one man. He is an Imagineer Extraordinaire."

DAVE SMITH
Chief Archivist Emeritus of the Walt Disney Archives

"This anecdotal memoir by Disney Legend Rolly Crump shares never-before-told stories with such charm and candor that it is a 'must have' addition for every Disney fan's library."

JIM KORKIS
Disney Historian and author of *The Vault of Walt*

"I loved stepping back in time with Rolly Crump and learning about the development of such great Disneyland attractions as the Haunted Mansion and the Enchanted Tiki Room. He also paints a vivid and personal portrait of Walt Disney that I'm sure fans and admirers will savor as much as I did."

LEONARD MALTIN
Disney Historian and Film Critic

Rolly's Acknowledgements

I would like to thank a few people who have helped me over the years.

Fanny Marie Fargo, my grandmother, for passing on her artistic, creative and funky spirit.

Candice Elizabeth Ivie, my Mom, for her absolute, undying love and support.

To my family—Leona, Roxanne, Chris and Theresa . . . Thank you for always letting Rolly be Rolly.

To my grand kids—Holly, Tyler and Todd . . . This is for you. Love Papa.

Walt Disney, the Old Man himself, for being my mentor and allowing me to be different.

All of the fine artists in Animation in the 1950s, who unknowingly became my teachers.

Bob McLain, because without him, this book would be no more than a few handwritten yellow lined pages in a notebook turning even more yellow with age since 2004. Thank you, Bob, for allowing me to share my stories with your website audience. Special thanks for introducing me to Jeff.

Jeff, obviously there would be no book without you and your incredible talent and interest in all things Disney. Thank you for devoting the last 2 years to this project and for being so faithful to the never-ending "cute" stories that filled your recorder. You're an "adopted grandson" to be proud of.

I also have to acknowledge the three things that helped me develop my imagination: the radio (for those of you that don't know, that was TV without pictures), magic and the comic strips.

JEFF'S ACKNOWLEDGEMENTS

Obviously, this book could not have happened without the help of many people who deserve to be thanked for everything they have done for me.

First off, a big thank you to my parents, Richard and Michele, and my brother, Justinn, for always being so supportive with everything I do.

Thank you to my wonderful fiancée, Martina Gona and her equally wonderful son, Alex, who have loved and supported me through every step of this endeavor…even when they hated me for getting to go to Disneyland without them!

Thank you to George Taylor, for being my Disney partner-in-crime, for offering invaluable advice, and for being one of the best friends a guy could have. Now that these shenanigans are over, we can start on one of our million other project ideas.

Thank you to Leonard Kinsey, who championed this project from the very beginning, and was always a huge help to me, not just in a publishing aspect, but also by being a damn good friend.

Thanks to my ever vigilant editor, Hugh Allison, who, while a stern taskmaster, made this book a hell of a lot better!

There are a few folks who pre-read the book before it got to the editing stage, offering invaluable advice, so thanks to David Younger, Josh Spiegel, and Estelle Hallick.

Bob McLain has my eternal gratitude, because without him this project would have never fallen into my lap to begin with, so thanks for that, Bob!

Also, a big thank you to the various people who helped contribute to the book in some form or another, whether it be through extra information, photos, or a nudge in the right direction: Bob Gurr, John Horny, Richard Harris, Jim Hill, Ken Kebow, Chris Crump, Christopher Merritt, Jim Korkis, and Dave Smith.

And last, but most certainly not least, a big thank you to Rolly and Marie for welcoming me into their lives with such open arms, being two of the most wonderful people I have ever met (or ever will meet, for that matter!), and allowing me to help tell the story of Rolly's life. You guys are the best "adopted grandparents" that a guy could ask for!

CONTENTS

FOREWORD BY BOB GURR 9

FOREWORD BY JOHN HORNY 10

CHAPTER 1: A BIT OF AN INTRODUCTION 13

CHAPTER 2: GROWING UP 15

CHAPTER 3: STARTING AT DISNEY 25

CHAPTER 4: DISNEYLAND 39

CHAPTER 5: MOVING TO WED 41

CHAPTER 6: THE HAUNTED MANSION 49

CHAPTER 7: ADVENTURELAND BAZAAR 53

CHAPTER 8: THE ENCHANTED TIKI ROOM 59

CHAPTER 9: THE 1964-1965 NEW YORK WORLD'S FAIR 65

CHAPTER 10: IT'S A SMALL WORLD AT DISNEYLAND 75

CHAPTER 11: MUSEUM OF THE WEIRD 85

CHAPTER 12: TOMORROWLAND RE-DESIGN 1967 93

CHAPTER 13: DISNEY ON PARADE 97

CHAPTER 14: SUPERVISING ART DIRECTOR AT DISNEYLAND 101

CHAPTER 15: WALT DISNEY WORLD 107

CHAPTER 16: CIRCUS WORLD 111

CHAPTER 17: KNOTT'S BEAR-Y TALES AT KNOTT'S BERRY FARM 115

CHAPTER 18: BACK AT DISNEY 123

CHAPTER 19: STEVE WYNN 131

CHAPTER 20: THE COUSTEAU SOCIETY 135

CHAPTER 21: OMAN 143

CHAPTER 22: DESIGN 27 149

CHAPTER 23: OTHER THEME PARKS 155

CHAPTER 24: RECENT WORK 161

CHAPTER 25: WALT 171

CHAPTER 26: LIFE REFLECTIONS 177

AFTERWORD 181

ROLAND F. CRUMP 183

ABOUT THE AUTHORS 189

DEDICATIONS

For Marie, whose love and support has meant more to me than I can ever put into words. —R.C.

For Mom and Nana, who instilled a love of Disney in me at an early age. Love you guys! —J.H.

FOREWORD

BY BOB GURR

When you've been friends with a co-worker for more than a half century, you do have observations. My dear friend and fellow legendary Imagineer Roland Fargo Crump, Jr. will now get the attention herewith. But it's plain Rolly from here onwards.

Rolly—there's nothing plain about Rolly. He's a guy who's indelible the moment you meet him—and indelible forever after. Picture this: an all breed dog kennel of thousands. One puppy stands out. The one that leaps highest for the dangled treat. The one that flashes unbridled enthusiasm. And the one that runs the farthest fastest when thrown the ball. And also the one that always returns reliably with the best answer to a challenge—that's Rolly.

Now you may think you are about to curl up with a nice book about a famous guy. Oh no—you just agreed to pull up a chair, pour Rolly a glass of wine, and be transported back in time. This book you will not read. You will listen mesmerized and enchanted as Rolly tells you an endless stream of cute stories. As he received his window on Main Street at Disneyland, when asked if he had a few words, he replied "If I get started, we'll all be here until next Tuesday." So beware, he's going to start—and he'll never stop.

Working with Rolly on some show improvements in the Devil scene at Disneyland's Mr. Toad's Wild Ride in 1956, I first met the Indelible Man. More than just a stylistic artist, he had a quick grasp of the physical realities of mechanical equipment. He artist, me mechanical man. This started a career-long association where I picked up so much art from him, and he picked up the mechanical stuff from me. Sort of a functional crisscross. His influence on my artistic expressions exceeds that of any person I've ever met.

Example: visitors to my home are struck by what a crazy colorful funky place I live in. More than one guest has said "so Crump-like." Indeed, I have some of Crump's art sculptures, and pristine copies of Rolly's infamous doper posters. He always decorated his workspace as an enclosed cave or hut, always with a big market umbrella. Nothing served any purpose—it was all in fun. My home today is "Crump."

He's always been that kind of visual environmental influence to all who know him.

Influence? Walt sure picked up on Rolly's whimsical and imaginative creations. A lot of folks were a bit reserved around Walt, but not Rolly. Oh no, Rolly had complete faith in his designs and would defend them to Walt in front of the other Imagineers to their discomfort. Remember that leaping puppy? Yeah—Rolly.

Rolly has the best stories about working with Walt better than any book by anyone who was ever there. Walt had a special affection for Rolly—that cute little tail wagging puppy. You will learn more about Walt, while the stories are supposed to be more about Rolly. This affection was absolutely genuine, no pander, no gushing. Imagine how efficient it was to work that way. No games, just create.

So dear reader, you'd better get set for a very long session. Once you start, neither of you will be able to stop.

FOREWORD

By John Horny

As with many of you who are about to read this book, I'd heard of Rolly Crump years before I met him. I was working at a small theme park in Northern California with a former Disney colleague of Rolly's where he told of Crump's varied body of work on the Dalmatians' spots, the Museum of the Weird and Small World. I saw his picture with Walt in just about every Disney book available at the time.

I had also heard other stories of him, driving in his Porsche late at night, screaming through the twisting roads of the Hollywood Hills, scaring the hippies! "You could hear him coming up the hill from Ventura Boulevard way before you'd ever see him," is what they used to say.

He had become mythic. The exemplar Imagineer! Independently minded, he had earned his stripes coming up through the ranks with his own self-made skills.

He had new, different, hip, cool, ingenious and often "weird" ideas. He did all the work from concept to installation with his own hands. He brought these ideas to life with an understanding of how they're made under the surface, what makes an idea tick (and tock). And he always did it with a sense of humor, creativity and fun…right up to the point of the first guest's contact with what he had created.

I started at WED in 1980 during a hiring frenzy that sucked up any half-talent available, and was lucky enough to work directly with Rolly on my first assignment.

"Working directly" is the only way you work with Rolly. He held no long-winded meetings, and no assistants delivered his notes. He carried the project with him in his head. He'd dash around the buildings to all the various designers, architects, model makers, and stylists, making small adjustments here, adding or subtracting a little there, "plussing" it every step of the way.

But more than anything, he constantly charged us up with his own enthusiasm, encouragement and, of course, by sharing his fabulous stories along the way, helping to pollinate our imaginations! He would never tell you that you had done something wrong, but instead would show you how to do it a little better. These little touches helped make it part of the story he was telling, and opened the door for your own creativity.

My first assignment was to paint the signs that were to hang in The Land pavilion's food court; the Farmers Market in EPCOT. These signs were very big, the largest being over 20 feet long, and beautifully sculpted in wood. All the colors Rolly chose were custom mixes of his own design. We established a routine where he would stop in every couple of days to check on the colors and my progress.

I was painting them at the back end of the WED model shop, which was a place Rolly obviously knew well. When he came into the shop, there was always a commotion; a shouted hello, a loud slap on someone's back, a burst of laughter, and so on. He'd always stop to talk and joke with old friends he had known from his Studios days and the very beginning of WED, such as Harriet Burns, Fred Joerger, Jack Ferges, Malcolm Cobb, Lee Toombs, Eddie Johnson, and many more. The shop was his stomping grounds. He made his entrance known, so I always knew he was coming.

This delay would just serve to make me even more nervous.

As he approached one morning, I quickly popped open a can of custom mixed paint, put the lid on a stool, and started making a swatch for review. I turned around just as Rolly sat down on that very stool with the lid on it.

I screamed! He screamed! He jumped up, *butt* it was too late. Right smack in the center of his pants was a perfect bullseye of custom mixed paint.

The whole shop was now looking at what that new kid had done to Rolly! I started to wipe at the mess, which only made it bigger and must have made it look even worse. Rolly asked for my smock to wrap around him and slipped off his pants so I could take them to the sink.

Then he actually started laughing. Not just laughing, but he was in hysterics. He had a big presentation to give to the top brass, and thought it the funniest thing in the world to do it without any pants!

I will never forget standing at that sink, crazily embarrassed, trying to clean this mess I had made on one of the Company's biggest, most senior, chief designers…and then looking over my shoulder at him to find him laughing as he walked out of the shop to meet some corporate sponsor without his pants.

That's Rolly…unforgettable!

That may be a personal story for me, but it shows how all the stories you are about to read have shaped not only me, but all the other people Rolly has touched in his life.

These stories, which appear to be bits of a life well lived, have all come back to me after reading this book. Having 30 years of my own life to reflect back on them, I have come to realize that many of my own experiences were shaped by these tales. They have kept me from losing my mind (or at least my sense of humor) whenever I have run into obstacles, mediocre minds, or a new kid who goofed up only to give me some reason to laugh.

So when you read these stories, you'll hear Rolly's voice…and I can vouch that it will sound just like when he told them to me. Take them into your life and use them as parables for the obstacles you'll run into, and remember that with creativity, resourcefulness, and a sense of fun and wonder, the world and your own stories will be that much better. That's Rolly's best story.

Me on Main Street, U.S.A. at Disneyland.

CHAPTER 1

A Bit of an Introduction

What you're holding in your hands is my life story. Over 80 years' worth of tales. It's crazy to think that it's all contained in here, isn't it?

Well, maybe not all of it. I remember so many stories that it's possible I left out a few. But those that made it in are definitely the best ones. The ones I cherish most.

Thinking now about the things I did, I sometimes feel like it's not a lot, but it really is.

I worked on and off with The Walt Disney Company for over 40 years.

I worked on my own for over 20 years.

I did work for Walt Disney, the Sultan of Oman, Steve Wynn, Jacques Cousteau, the Knotts family, and so many more.

I traveled the world and back again.

My work varied from the grandest of attractions to the smallest of details.

And I feel very fortunate that I was able to do every single one of them.

Of all the things that I've done, how could you possibly fit it all into a book?

My whole life is based on a bunch of wonderful, crazy little stories.

Every story I tell is a little kinky, and kind of funny.

If you get the audience to laugh, they'll continue to listen to you.

Hopefully, what's contained in these pages does make you laugh, and you'll enjoy it right up until the very end.

So, you want to hear the tale of Rolly Crump?

Well, it's kind of a cute story…

CHAPTER 2

GROWING UP

In the 1920s, a lovely woman named Candice Elizabeth Ivie met a man called Roland Fargo Crump. They fell in love, and got married soon after. On Feb 27th 1930, in Alhambra, California, their little bundle of joy arrived in the form of me, Roland Fargo Crump, Jr.

It was a happy marriage, except that when the Wall Street Crash hit, my Dad lost his job. By the time I was 5, we were living in Redlands, California, and my Dad was having a really rough time. He had graduated from college and everything, but that just couldn't help him find any work. Eventually, he got a job in a liquor store. He only worked there for a short period of time, but it was long enough to create a problem that would eventually end the marriage.

It was around that time that my Mom told me that all we had to our name was a single dime. My Dad was drinking away his pay, and we had nothing. She went to Downtown Redlands, and got a job at a department store to help support us.

My Mom took me and moved in with her parents in Eagle Rock, California. I spent a lot of years there, growing up with my grandparents, who were a real sweet couple, while my Mom went out to find jobs anywhere she could. She tried her best to not move me around all the time, but I still ended up going to 6 grammar schools. When you're a little guy with no brothers or sisters, you're scared shitless every time you're the new guy at school! But, somehow, we made it work.

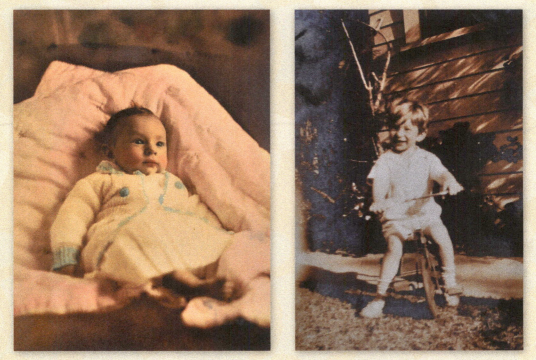

Left: Here's me, little Roland Fargo Crump, Jr. at 11 weeks old. • *Right:* A much younger me riding my bicycle. • *Opposite:* A much younger me playing out in the garden.

To be honest with you, I was never an unhappy child. I was never upset, mad or anything like that. I think that's mostly because art was my outlet and kept me together. I had always loved drawing, ever since I was 2 years old, but as time went on, it really became a sort of crutch. I was able to create these things from inside my mind, and I could just get lost in them for hours. Listening to the radio helped with that a lot, too. I used to listen to it every afternoon, for 2-3 hours at a time. The shows were only 15 minutes long, things like *Jack Armstrong* and *The Shadow*, but they helped give me this great imagination. I got involved in magic shortly after that. That really blew my little mind, because I'd see a trick, and immediately try to figure out how it was done. The combination of magic, radio and drawing all melded together and helped shaped me as a person. I was a happy little guy.

A lot of people ask me if there were any other artists in my family. I have always said no, because I never really thought of anyone in my family as an artist until years later. The truth is, though, that I really did have some marvelous artists in my family, going all the way back to the 1800s.

My great-grandmother, Marie Fargo, studied art over in Paris. She spent some time over there when she was a young woman, and did some gorgeous oil paintings. I still have a beautiful little painting that she did of some roosters.

Fanny Marie Fargo, my grandmother, studied at the Art Institute of Chicago. She did some wonderful things. I'm a lot like her, in that she was very versatile with her work. I remember she hand carved this little wooden box, which was used to hold playing cards. She made it around 1870 and, luckily, I still have it. It's a gorgeous little box for such a simple thing.

I remember she was getting up there in years, but lived in a barn out in the middle of an orange grove that she owned in California. I think she was about 88 years old when I went to visit her one time, and a lot of her artwork was in a tent nearby. She had lived in that tent for years before moving into the barn, but she still kept a lot of her personal possessions in it. I was a teenager then, only about 15, and I was being a good grandson by going to check in on her. I remember the tent was starting to tear, and there was this pile of her worldly possessions getting exposed to the weather. That gorgeous little box was sitting on top of the pile. I was afraid it was going to get damaged, so I did what any kid my age would have done; I stole it from her!

One of my earliest drawings of Popeye.

Well, the next time I went up to see her, she said to me, "Did you steal my card box?"

"No, grandma I didn't," I said to her.

"Are you sure?" she asked me.

"I'm positive," I replied.

"Well, it's gone," she said, kind of disappointed. She loved that thing, too.

Thinking quick on my feet, I said, "Well, you gave it to me. Don't you remember?" She used to complain about the fact that her memory wasn't as good as it used to be, so I used that to my advantage. She was just glad to know where it was, and I got to keep the box safe in my hands. It still is one of my most prized possessions. I like to think that a lot of her creativity seeped into me because I was spending so much time with her.

Anyway, getting back to my art, I loved to draw growing up, and I still have this beautiful little book of drawings that I did when I was very young. My mother kept it safe, and I'm glad she did, because it really showed what an artist I used to be when I was 2 years old.

My mother always encouraged me with my art, which was im-portant to me. She was very proud of it, and I think that helped me out a lot while developing my style. My Mom was one of the most important people in my life because she always supported me in everything I wanted to do. A lot of times, if a kid wants to be an artist, their parents try to sway them out of it. Sometimes they think artists won't be able to sustain themselves. But my Mom

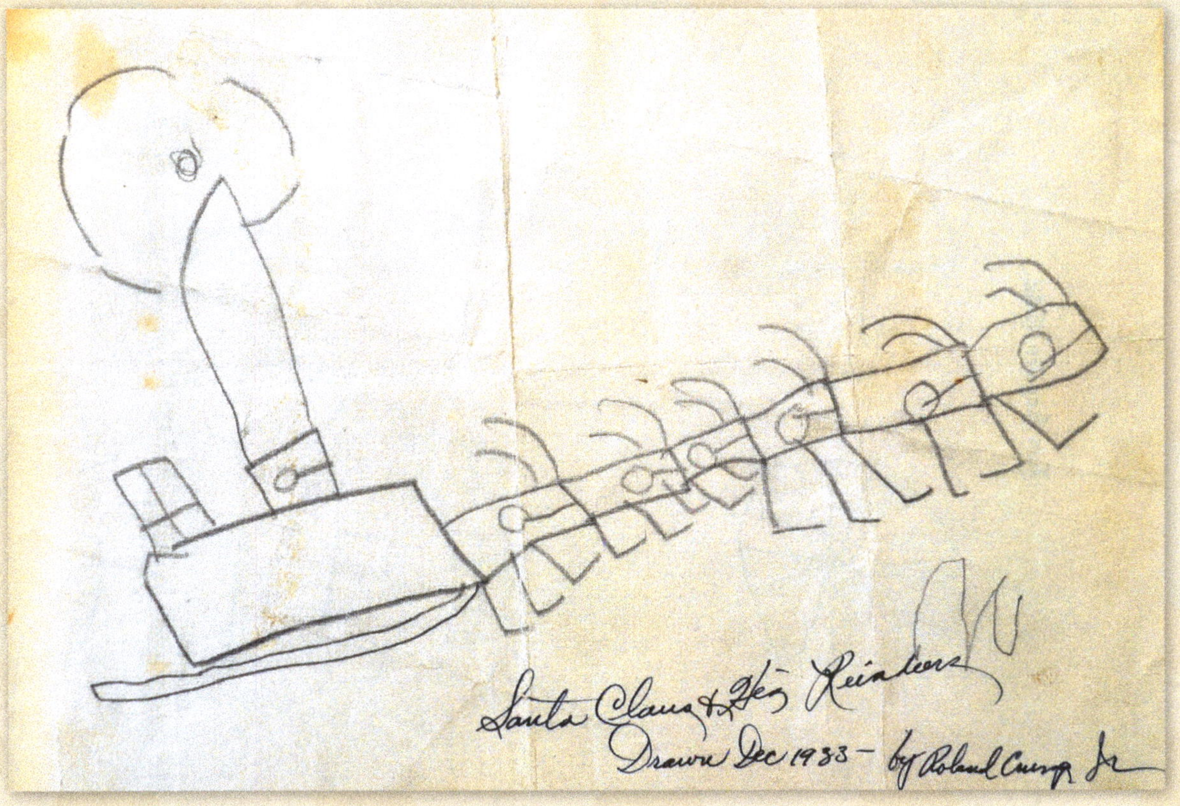

*Santa Claus & His Reindeers
Drawn Dec 1933 — by Roland Curry Jr*

Above: My drawing of Santa Claus from 1933.
Below: My drawing from 1935 of the boxing match that I drew immediately after I got home before I would go to bed.

*Max Baer
Joe Louis Fight
Oct 1935*

The Ring-Siders

was aware of my active imagination and how much I wanted to be an artist, so she always supported me in whatever I wanted to do.

In the little book that I have, I drew Santa Claus and his reindeer. If you looked at it now, you wouldn't have a freaking clue what it was! But my mother, in her infinite wisdom, wrote "Santa Claus and his reindeer" on it to help keep a record of her budding young artist. That book covers a lot of my work from the time I was 2 years old up until I was 5. It's a treasure, really, and probably why I started keeping scrapbooks of all the projects I worked on throughout my life.

I remember one time when we had gone to a movie, the newsreel they showed beforehand was of a big boxing match that had just taken place. When we got home, I went over to my pen and paper and announced that I had to draw it. My Mom said, "No, honey, it's time for you to go to bed."

"No, I have to draw it," I insisted. So, I drew a picture of the two boxers fighting, because the image was so clear in my head. It's funny, because the two fighters had their initials on their shorts. I didn't remember what letters they were exactly, but I put initials on the drawing anyway, showing that I paid attention to those small details. My Mom said that I wouldn't go to bed until I'd drawn it!

I obviously continued drawing beyond that. In fact, they had a contest when I was in junior high, looking to see who could draw the best Santa Claus. So, I did a Santa Claus drawing and entered it. I thought it was really ugly, honestly, but I won the award anyway! I remember thinking, 'Oh, I guess I'm doing it right after all!'

**A few drawings from
my early 20s.**

IT'S KIND OF A CUTE STORY

As soon as I'd get home from school every day, I'd sit and draw while waiting for my mother to come home from work. I did all kinds of pictures, but I was mostly influenced by the comic strips. Things such as *Red Ryder*, *Prince Valiant* and the superheroes. At one time, I had the very first Superman comic book and the first Batman comic book. I kept those books for years and years, then I finally threw them away. I kick myself now for that, not realizing what they were going to mean all these years later.

I would sit and trace them, though. I would trace Superman and Batman in action, and I would just have piles of this artwork that I copied straight from the books. It helped me get a feel for the human body, too, no matter how exaggerated it may have been in those books. It's a habit that I've had for years, and it has really has helped me along the way. With artists whose work that I really loved, I would trace a piece of something they did just to get a feel for it. In a way, I was constantly educating myself by doing this, and learning new techniques. As I grew older, I talked to other artists and they said they did the same thing. Anyway, that's basically what I did up through high school as well. I did go to Chouinard Art Institute for six Saturdays when I was 16, but that's it. That's the only formal art training I had.

Overall, I felt that a lot of things about art you had to learn on your own. No one can teach you talent, let alone what looks good for your particular style. Teachers can screw that up for their students sometimes. They'd tell me never put red and green together, except when it was Christmas time. They said black and white are not actual colors. They used to tell me all these things, and I'd feel like telling them where to stick it! So, I lost interest in the formal stuff.

I had one teacher in high school that I really loved. She felt it was worth my time to do things over again. She made me do it 2, 3, even 4 times until she thought I had it down. That happened a lot when I worked in Animation at Disney, too. Having to do it again really teaches you how to hone your skill, and pay attention to the little details.

She realized that every student is different. You have to talk to them differently because everyone has different styles. You don't want to intimidate young artists. You find what they like doing most, and let them explore that. Don't make them do a project that would be hard for them to grasp. You have to get their confidence up first, and then nudge them along into these new areas. She taught me that, and I loved her for it. I always carried that lesson with me.

In high school, I did a lot of artwork for school functions. People would ask me to draw up a poster for dances, or to advertise something, and I always did it. I also did the artwork for the 'yell books.' Those were the programs they handed out at football games, and they had all the players listed. Finally, I did

Cover of my High School yell book.

artwork for my high school annual in 1947, which was pretty neat, too. So, I kept myself busy in high school. All of those drawings were done with ink, because that's what I learned from the comic strips when I was younger. It wasn't until later that I started to use color.

Like I said, my Mom was proud of me, and wanted me to do this art thing for a living. She felt I had a talent, and she wanted me to pursue it. She even wrote letters to Walt when I was 16, trying to get me a job with him! She thought it would be good if I could get paid for doing something I loved. Of course, it didn't quite work out that way yet. I grew up in a time where it was important to have a job at my age, even more so for someone in my position. I even had a full-time job when I was in high school. I worked 40 hours a week washing dishes, and still went to school. I helped support my Mom with that extra cash, just like she always supported me. I bought my own clothes, minus the socks, shorts, and underwear. My Mom still got those for me. But I gave her whatever little bits of money I had left over.

This page and opposite: **Interior designs from one of my high school annuals.**

IT'S KIND OF A CUTE STORY

After high school, I went out and got a job working at a ceramic factory. Again, this goes back to me wanting to help my mother out, and how important it was for me to have a job. I grew up coming out of the Great Depression, so I wanted to help in every little way I could. Not long after that, I met some kids that were going to Idaho to work in forestry there. I thought that sounded interesting, so when they asked if I wanted to go, I said sure.

I spent the whole summer working in blister rust control at Coeur d'Alene National Forest. Basically, there was a bush that carried pollen that killed white pine trees by giving it these awful blisters. It was our job to go in there and kill the bushes that destroyed the white pines.

One of the other guys I worked with was from Oklahoma. When you're working with these guys side by side, pulling out bad bushes on the mountain day in, day out, you start to pick up their little mannerisms. He had a thick accent, so by the end of the first week, I had this Southern accent. He said to me, "Are you from the South?"

"No, goddamn it," I said. "It's from working with you! I picked it up!"

Eventually, I made my way back home, and started working at the ceramic factory again. I was happy working there, doing my little sketches on the side. But I always wanted more. And soon, I was going to get it.

**This page and opposite:
A few drawings from my early 20s.**

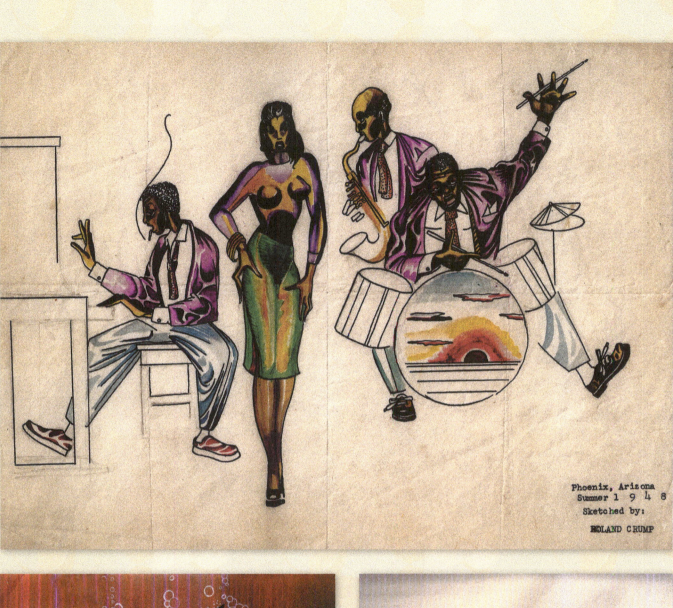

Phoenix, Arizona
Summer 1 9 4 8
Sketched by:
ROLAND CRUMP

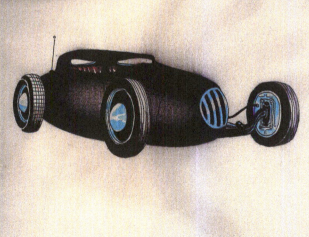

CHAPTER 3

STARTING AT DISNEY

Bck in 1951, my mother and I had Christmas dinner with some friends of hers. It turned out that one of the ladies present worked in Animation at the Disney Studios. Of course, from the time I was a little kid, I wanted to work for Disney. I mean, every artist at that time wanted to. I remember when my Dad took me to the theater to see *The Three Little Pigs* when it was first released. I couldn't have been more than 3 or 4 years old. I was aware of Disney because of the cartoons in the newspaper, but when I saw it, I was blown away. I knew from that moment that I wanted to work for Walt. I never thought it would actually happen, but I was a little kid with a dream.

I told this lady all of that and said I would love to work there someday. She was so nice, and told me exactly who to contact to get the gears in motion. So the very next day, I called this guy, Andy Engman, and asked for an interview. Luckily, he said yes.

I went for the interview, but I was absolutely scared to death. I really didn't have a clue what to expect. I gave them my portfolio, they asked me a few questions, and then they made me take an animation test. The good news was I was used to handling a pencil by that point, which helped me a lot.

Believe it or not, I showed them my high school art portfolio when they asked for some samples of my artwork. I thought it was just fine at the time but years later, when I moved out of Animation and into WED, I was informed that I had the worst portfolio of anyone that ever applied for a job in Animation. How I was actually hired I have no idea but they must have seen something in my work!

After the test, they took me upstairs to the personnel department and said, "Well, we'd like to possibly hire you."

"My God, really?" I said. "That would be great! How much would I start at?"

"Oh, we'd start you at $30 a week."

I didn't know what to say. At the time, I was making $75 a week working at a ceramic factory as a dipper! It was a huge pay cut. I told them I had to sleep on it, and I'd call them in the morning.

I went home, and talked to my Mom about it. They were offering me less than half the salary I was already making! I was pretty nervous about that. But my mother, in her wisdom, looked at me and said, "Honey, you always wanted to go work for Disney. Just go for it."

Again, that shows how much my Mom supported me, and wanted me to pursue what I wanted to do. So, I just went for it, like she told me to. I called them up the next day and said, "Yes, I'd like the job."

What's interesting, though, is that I continued to work on the weekends at another job, making sewer manholes (from the holes themselves to the covers), so I could afford to live.

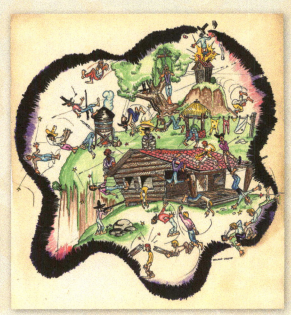

Right and opposite: **Drawings from my portfolio that I submitted to Disney.**

This page and opposite: Drawing from my portfolio that I submitted to Disney.

Monday through Friday, I worked for Disney. But every Saturday and Sunday, I was lowering bricks and mixing mud for a friend of mine. It's funny, though, because I made $40 working for him. I was making more money on the weekends than in my entire week at Disney! I didn't mind, though, because I loved going to work every day, and just being at the Disney Studios was like being in Heaven.

So I started there in 1952 as an inbetweener. In fact, I was the last inbetweener hired to work on *Peter Pan*. In case you don't know what that is, an inbetweener is the guy who does every other drawing. In animation, there are 24 frames a second, so that translates to 24 drawings a second. So, as an inbetweener, I was doing 12 of those 24 frames.

As time went on, I became an assistant animator, where I learned to run the movieola, which was a small machine used to view film reels. Back in the 1950s, they still shot tests for each scene. For example, an animator would do a scene, but it would be just a test, more like a rough scene. He would do one frame, his assistant would do one frame, and the inbetweener would do one frame. This process would go on until the scene was complete. They would send it to the camera department, who would make a loop of that scene. The camera department would bring it back to the animator, who would study it to see what he liked and what he didn't like. He might say, "Make some changes there" or he might say nothing at all. When you really stop to think about it, they spent a lot of money on animation back then. They spent all this money on those tests, to make sure everything was total perfection. It was absolutely unbelievable. You'd never see that today.

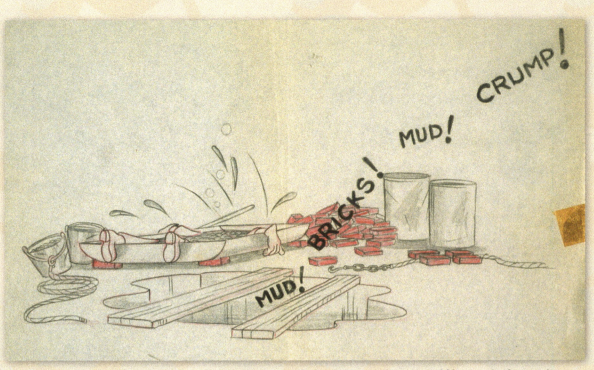

My job on the weekends was to help make sewer manholes, but sometimes I would be too tired to work!

From there, the tests would go to clean-up. That meant that all the rough drawings were cleaned up and made into these real, crisp drawings. After that, they were sent to Ink and Paint, where they were put on cels to eventually be filmed and put into the film itself. It was a long, expensive process but back then Disney really spared no expense for animation.

When we were doing *101 Dalmatians*, I remember that the animators all got together and had an interesting talk that kind of led to a new technique. The thing was, when you looked at a rough scene, it was far better than the cleaned up scene, because it had all these lines that came across as living breathing things. It's hard to explain, really, but to us, the rough scenes almost always looked better than the final, cleaned up ones.

Overall, though, my Animation résumé at Disney isn't all that vast. It only includes *Peter Pan*, *Lady and the Tramp*, *Sleeping Beauty* and *101 Dalmatians*. It was such a great time in my life, though, and I really learned an awful lot there.

Like I mentioned earlier, they weren't paying me a lot, so I always had to do a few things on the side to make a couple of bucks. When I really think about it, one of the reasons I got so damn creative was because I had to make some money. That's how my crystal radios came about.

Back in the 1920s, they used to have these crystal radios, which were basically little radios that you could make out of a crystal. They were small little units, usually with an alligator clip attached so you could ground it. On the end of them was this little earphone, and you adjusted it little by little until you picked up some kind of signal. They still sell kits of them today, but back then, they were made from whatever you could find.

Anyway, there was a fellow in Animation who was making these. There were two stations in San Fernando that had a pretty strong signal that could be picked up by these things, so it was worth it. In Animation, you really couldn't listen to the radio at your desk because you didn't want to disturb the people working around you. So, these little things became a good source of entertainment for folks who wanted a little music in their day.

I thought it was one of the neatest damn things I'd ever seen, and wanted to make one for myself. Now, this guy was making them and putting them in these plastic pill boxes. I thought that was kind of boring, and wanted to get a little more creative with it.

I got a walnut, and took everything out of it. There was just enough room for the crystal radio set, so I managed to squeeze one in there. I spruced it up a bit, making it a little more fancy, and called it "My Nutty Radio." People seemed to like them, because they kept asking me to make them one. I sold a whole bunch of them. It costs me about $2.50 for all the components, but then I turned around and sold them for $5 apiece.

IT'S KIND OF A CUTE STORY

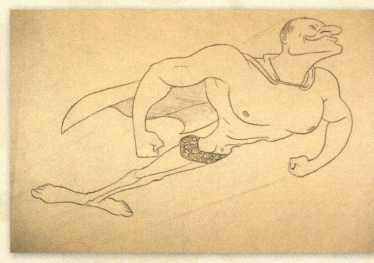

Super Crump caricature.

I made a nice profit off of them!

It was kind of cute, because a few folks from the personnel department bought them, but they complained that they got horrible reception in their office. Always one for customer service, I went up on the roof with a little roll of wire. I attached it to the building with pushpins, and then lowered the wire down to their window. Then, I attached all of their little antennas to that wire, and voila… perfect reception!

I remember going to the sweat box an awful lot. A sweat box was where you would go to watch the segments of the film that you were working on. They would almost always have an audience there to check it out as well. At the end of each screening, which would usually contain about five minutes worth of footage, they would give the audience a little card to fill out, asking all sorts of questions. Who was your favorite character? Do you think they were the right size and shape? They really quizzed everyone about the characters and the scenes. Walt would read those damn things and, if there was some suggestion in there that he felt was really worthwhile, he'd have us go back and reanimate it. Obviously, that cost a bit of money, not to mention took more time, but to Walt, it was worth it. So, like I said earlier, the strive for perfection was absolutely unbelievable.

To get back on subject again, I remember going to one of those sweat box sessions, and laughing like I'd never laughed before. They were showing an unused sequence of Captain Hook being swallowed by the crocodile from *Peter Pan*, all of it done in rough animation, and it was just hilarious. The whole place completely came undone.

The animators knew that the rough animation got some things across that the final version couldn't, because there was nothing sharp about the film. It was just wild…flat out wild. The roughness of it really added something that was lost in translation later on. When we were doing *101 Dalmatians*, they decided that they were going to try something new. Instead of taking all their drawings to Ink and Paint, they used to Xerox them. The animators thought that would be a good way to incorporate some of the rough drawings into the actual film. Then, once a scene was Xeroxed, they put it on the cels. After that, then they went to Ink and Paint, but with the expressed notion that they were not to have defined lines. In fact, the backgrounds in *101 Dalmatians* were all line drawings that were put over color slates. They didn't try to render the buildings, so they were reaching out to this new technology. It was interesting, because a lot of the things that were in that particular film were taken right off the rough drawings.

Just before that, I started working as the assistant animator to Eric Larson. Now, a lot of you will recognize him as being one of the fabled "Nine Old Men." But, in case you don't know who the "Nine Old Men" are, they were the core group of animators who helped create some of Disney's most famous cartoons. Walt jokingly referred to them by that name as a reference to the book *The Nine Old Men* by Robert Allen and Drew Pearson, about the nine justices of the Supreme Court.

Anyway, Eric was such a sweetheart to work for. He was absolutely a delight and we got along beautifully. He supported

"HMM… WHICH ONE SHOULD I WEAR TODAY?"

My intense workout regimen and my muscles were often the subject of poking fun.

me in everything I did and was a great teacher, too. I really learned a lot from him. Again, I had no formal training, so if anything, I learned from The School of Eric Larson.

It was funny how I wound up working for him, though. I was working on *Sleeping Beauty* at the time, and did clean-up on a scene. After I was finished, it went off to the director and some of the other head animators for review. I heard a little while later that Eric, who was one of the sequence directors, didn't like my clean-up on it.

"Oh my God," I said. "I might as well quit the Company now!" Eric was one of those guys that everyone looked up to, because even back then, he was a legend in Animation. I figured if he didn't like what I did, I didn't have a shot anymore. It turns out though he just had a few pointers for me to correct, and he asked me to be his assistant. I was very surprised by that!

I always thought he was a sweetheart. He was Mormon, and had strong ties to the Church. He donated a percentage of his salary every month to the Church, which I thought was very nice of him. He also dressed just like a banker. Every day, he wore a three-piece suit with a tie. He was immaculate.

Caricature of me, made by some of my friends in Animation.

He used to take care of me, too. He knew I'd get frustrated working there from time to time, and that I wasn't happy with the amount of money I was making. So, he'd always go in and tell them what a great job I was doing and recommend me for a raise. He really knew how to keep me going.

I always repaid the favor, too. When he was depressed, I'd ask him what kind of music he wanted to hear, and play his favorite stations. I'd get him sparkling water, order it by the case, and take care of the bill for him. When he was stressed, I'd calm him down with a back massage. We just got along wonderfully.

I remember when we were working on *101 Dalmatians* together, he animated all the puppies in that one sequence where they're watching television. When the scenes came back from rough, he handed them to me and said, "Okay Rolly, do the spots!" If you've seen the movie, you know that all of the dogs in it have spots. Lots and lots of spots! I had to animate all those individual spots on the puppies in that one sequence.

I forget how long the sequence ran in real time, but I was animating spots for six months! It was definitely a learning experience for me. You don't think about it when you're watching the movie, but I learned that when you put a spot on an animal, the spots have to move with them. If they reach out for something, the spot has to reach out, too. Not only that, but the spot has to stretch, so it stays in proportion with the rest of the body. It wasn't difficult to begin with, but imagine it on a dog that's running. And then imagine it on 101 dogs! That spot pretty much looks like it is opening and closing and opening and closing! Otherwise, it would just slide all over the place, and look ridiculous. That was a lot of work, but it came out as a gorgeous piece of animation.

Animation in general was such a nuts place, though. My God, the things these guys would do to each other was just crazy. They were one big family, and they all got along great, so they used to mess with each other all the time. They used to have tours go through the department, where they would bring people in from out of state to look around. There would usually be about 6 to 10 people on each tour, and they would come in and have one of the animators talk to them about how you do animation. They usually let us know ahead of time who was going to do the talking for that tour. As soon as the animators got that information, oh God, it was all set.

This one time, it was going to be Ward Kimball doing the talking. We had a little Japanese fellow, Iwao Takamoto, who was a real sweetheart, working there at the time. So Ward and Iwao worked out this plan to mess with the tour. Ward put Iwao in the closed closet in their room. The closet was big enough to just barely fit one person inside it. But Iwao went in, and the two of them worked out a little scene. Now, these six people from somewhere in Iowa came to Ward's office, and he's talking to them, and suddenly there is a knock

IT'S KIND OF A CUTE STORY

Goofing around with some of my Animation buddies.

on the closet door. The tour group was a little confused, but Ward acted like it wasn't strange in the slightest!

Ward goes, "Who is it?" and then a little voice from the closet goes, "Iwao!"

"Oh, Iwao! What a surprise! Yeah, I'll be right there." So Ward went over, and opens the door to what was very obviously the closet, and Iwao steps out. He had a scene in his hand that he handed over to Ward and said, "Ward, would you check the scene for me?"

Ward looked at it and went through it right there with him, going, "Yeah, make the eyebrow a little stronger there. And fix that up a little here. There, that's good!" When he was done going through the whole scene, he gave it back, and then Iwao went back in the closet and shut the door behind him. The real kicker is that the tour group was still in the room for another 20 minutes after that! Oh God, it was just hilarious. That's the extent that they would go to just to have some fun.

Another crazy story is that one night I was at the Studio working late on *Peter Pan*. I went to show these two assistants that I was working with something I had done, and when I came into their room, they were lying down on the floor. I had no idea what they were doing, and asked them. Turns out, they were drilling a hole in the wall.

In Animation at that time, the artists sat at a desk with a built-in light, so they could see what they were working on at all times. There was a little hole at the bottom of each desk for an electric cord for the light. These two guys were drilling a hole in the wall to match up to the hole on the other side.

Now, the room they were drilling into belonged to Milt Kahl, another one of the famous "Nine Old Men." He was great guy, and one of the leading animators for the Studio.

They finished drilling their hole, and put a little tube in it. Now, they were all set. Milt would sit down at the desk to work, and not suspect a thing. Once a week, for God knows how many weeks, they would take a big squeeze ball filled with talcum powder, and shoot it through the tube. Milt would get up to go to lunch, and there'd be talcum powder all over his crotch! Milt was kind of a noisy guy, and he would jump up and scream, "Jesus Christ!" The entire department would hear him. Meanwhile, these two were in a fit of giggles in the room right next to him.

Of course, when he'd look under the desk, they'd pull the little tube out and plug up the hole so he didn't see it. This went on for weeks and used to drive him nuts! He'd yell and scream, but for the life of him, he couldn't figure out where the talcum powder was coming from.

After the talcum powder trick got old, they started collecting flies in a jar. They hooked it up to the tube, and kept tapping this jar full of flies every so often. The flies would keep coming up from underneath the desk, and Milt would start yelling about the fly infestation that seemingly came from nowhere.

Well, one day Milt was going to have lunch with Walt over in the Coral Room, the commissary at the Studios. The guys knew about this, and decided to step up their prank a little bit. So Milt had on a sport coat and tie that day to look nice for the boss. You could tell when someone was going to leave, because they would turn off their light on the table. Because it had a metal base, it would make this big bang every time

"WOULD YOU LIKE TO SEE MY LATEST TRICK?"

Cartoon someone drew of me, showing how easy it was for me to charm the women at the Disney Studios.

you turned it off. As soon as he hit the light switch, they let Milt have it with hot water, and completely wiped out his entire crotch. Here he is, about to go to have lunch with Walt, and his whole crotch is just sopping wet. Of course, he's yelling and screaming and he runs next door to find these two in a laughing fit. He finally realizes what those guys have been up to the whole time, and boy, did he let them have it!

Luckily, I wasn't on the receiving end of too many practical jokes. I think the worst I got was when they would tape down the switch hook on the telephone. The switch hook was the part that the receiver held down when the phone was 'on the hook.' Once you picked up the phone, the switch hook would come up, letting the phone realize that someone was trying to make or take a call. So the phone would ring, and I would pick it up to answer it, but it would just keep ringing because someone had taped down the switch hook. It always took me a while to figure that one out!

Animation was an interesting place to work, though. Sure, it was a lot of fun, but I also saw some of its bad side while working there as well. I learned a lot about jealousy during my time there, believe it or not.

At the time, Mary Blair was the only female painter who had done backgrounds for Disney, and everything she did was very stylistic. Walt loved the way her work looked, so he would make sure that whatever background she did, the animated characters would fit her style. A lot of the guys didn't like that so much. They got a little jealous because he'd make them change their style to fit in with hers. Most of the animators were used to using a style that Ward Kimball called the "moldy fig" method.

What he was referring to by that phrase was any type of animation that looked like it was done in the 1930s by Disney. You know the kind; looking old-fashioned, like Mickey Mouse with three stripes on his gloves. It was his way of trying to make a distinction between the old way, and the more stylized animation he was trying to get Walt to do. *Snow White*, *Pinocchio*, all those old features, despite making lots of money, were considered "moldy figs" because they were done using the old methods. That's not really a term that was heard outside of the animation studio, and I'm sure I'm one of the last guys left now that even remembers it!

When Mary came in, and started doing these stylized drawings, the animators got a little perturbed because they had to change to match her. They preferred using the "moldy fig" method, but Walt made them change their ways a bit. That was the thing with Walt, though. He would find somebody that had a talent that he really liked, and he'd want to use it as much as he could.

It was certainly an education working there, too, because I was put in a bullpen with 4 or 5 other people when I first started. Sure, they were all animators, but on their own time, they were real artists. They did their own painting, sculpting, and all sorts of stuff. While I was working with them, I picked up a lot of other talents that I never would have learned otherwise. Those guys I shared the bullpen with were the best teachers I ever had.

I started to get excited about all of this stuff. I never knew who Henri de Toulouse-Lautrec or Picasso were before. But all of a sudden, I was learning all this through osmosis. A whole new world was opened up to me, and what I learned from those guys was really the foundation of my entire career from that point on.

There was a fellow by the name of Frank Armitage that brought a mobile he built into the office one day. It was no more than a coat hanger with some strings hanging down, then an eraser, with some more strings hanging down, with a pencil. It moved in the most beautiful way, because the pieces moved right past each other in this very strange way. I was fascinated by it. It was my first look at a kinetic sculpture.

"What is that?" I asked Frank.

"It's a mobile," he replied.

"What the hell's a mobile?" I asked him. I really had no idea. I had never seen anything like it before.

"Go to the library, and look up Alexander Calder," he told me. The Disney Studios had this incredible library filled with tons of books, so I did just that. I read everything I could on Calder, mobiles and kinetic sculptures. All of a sudden, I started building mobiles on the weekends when I had time off from my second job!

This went on for the next year and a half or so. I just built mobile after mobile after mobile. My house had mobiles hanging in every single room. My kids were still very young at the time, but they loved them, too. They knew how delicate they were, though, so they didn't bother the mobiles so much. I remember a salesman coming to the door one time, and he looked in the house while he was talking to my wife, and saw all the mobiles hanging.

"Obviously, you don't have any children," he said to her.

"Why do you say that?" she asked. "I have three!"

"But all these things hanging down, they don't get destroyed?" He was surprised! But she told him they knew their father would be very upset if any of them broke. They were wonderful, though, and I just loved making them.

I had to try out everything that all my co-workers did. I think it was similar to when I was a young kid, and was tracing comic books. I wanted to try everything. Two other fellows were painting on rocks in 1953, and sure enough, I started to do that, too. My grandmother used to do that as well, paint on stuff she found lying around her yard. These two other guys didn't do anything particularly spectacular with the rocks, but I started to embellish on them. The very first rock painting I ever did was of a little rooster. For being on a rock, it was pretty detailed. I just loved it so much, so I wound up doing a whole series of rock paintings.

I thought maybe I could have a rock tell a story, since no one else did anything like that before. I did one of Bluebeard with a little speech bubble that says, "I dig chicks." I decided to do Ben Franklin next. He had a good idea, which as you know, was to harness electricity, so my little rock story had Ben Franklin inventing the light bulb.

On another rock, I painted a cross-eyed Betsy Ross in front of an American flag, with the red and white stripes going the wrong way. The caption on that one read "Betsy, you goofed." On yet another rock, I had Tarzan and an ape in a staring contest, with the words "Me Tarzan, You Jane."

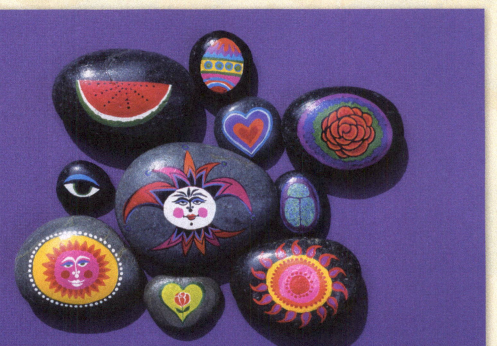

An assortment of my painted rocks.

Bluebeard: "I dig chicks."

Painted rock, showing Ben Franklin and his bright idea.

Betsy Ross, as depicted on one of my painted rocks.

I have a pencil in my "Disney Room" at home, and it's framed since it's very special to me, because that pencil changed my life. It sounds strange, but it's true.

There was a clip that held an eraser to that pencil. One of the other guys I worked with, Wathel Rogers, had taken the clip off of that pencil and made a little propeller out of it, balancing it on the top of a pushpin. Every time I went into his room, I would stare at it.

"Wathel, how did you do that?" I'd ask him every single time.

"I can't tell you!" This went on for weeks and weeks. Every day, I'd ask him, but the answer was always the same, "Oh no, it's a big secret. I can't reveal it."

Finally, I tried to make one of them myself because I just wanted to know. I used a nail to make a dent in another clip, and tried to balance it out. That obviously was not a good idea, because it came out crooked, and it didn't always hook onto the end right.

Eventually, Wathel broke down and said, "I'll tell you what; I'll sell you the secret for a penny." I was just thrilled! So I forked over the penny, and he leaned in real close and said, "You use a ballpoint pen to make the dent, so the dent is smooth."

I immediately ran back to my room to try it out. And sure enough, it worked! I was so proud that I'd finally made one. I found that, due to the air conditioning in the Studios, the propeller would spin on its own, which I thought was kind of neat.

One of the other guys came by one time, saw my little propeller, and asked how it worked. I wasn't going to torture him like Wathel did to me, so I told him how it worked. Well, he went back to his office, and made one of his own. I walked by a few days later and saw it, and I thought, 'Wait a second…his is bigger than mine!'

The pencil that I took the eraser clip from to make my very first propeller.

IT'S KIND OF A CUTE STORY

Tarzan, as depicted on one of my painted rocks.

I couldn't have that, so I went back to my office, and started making propellers that were bigger than his, with strings hanging off of them. I had little sticks that I glued together with pins up on top. I had 6 or 7 propellers like that, turning in the air conditioning. After that, to make sure he didn't outdo me again, I really went nuts with them. I had at least 30 of them at any given time, made out of all sorts of things. Some were inside wine bottles; some were on top of brandy snifters. The whole damn room was filled with them, and I was just having a ball.

I had this great big black mobile that was hanging in my office that I brought from home. I remember coming into my office one morning, and found it in pieces all over my floor and desk. There was this little note on the top of my desk that said "I'm sorry!" signed by the janitor.

He came in the night before to clean up a bit, and he didn't turn the light on right away. All of a sudden, while he was sweeping, he brushed up against that mobile, and he felt it touch his ear. He looked up and saw this black thing in the darkness, and he thought it was a gigantic spider!

He took his broom, and just beat the shit out of it! When he finally realized that it wasn't a spider, it was too late. It was in shambles. He found me shortly after that and apologized again. I told him it was fine, but we couldn't help but laugh at that! I managed to fix it up again, but I hung it on the opposite side of the room after that.

There was this one animator who was kind of a grouchy guy. He was never very positive about anything, and would always be crabby about one thing or another when he came in every morning. One day he walked past my office, and noticed one of my mobiles.

"Wow, what's that?" he said. I told him it was a mobile.

"Where did you get that?" he asked. I told him I made it.

"That is just gorgeous," he said, and he started to go on about it. Now, I have always believed in a lot of the old philosophies about life. There's this old Japanese custom that I always keep in my mind. In Japan, if you admire something that another person owns, that person is supposed to give it to you as a sign of good will.

Having kept that in mind, I said to him, "Do you really like it?" He said he did.

"Do you want it?" I asked him. He was surprised.

"If you really like it, I'll give it to you," I told him. He just melted. He couldn't believe it, and he couldn't thank me enough. From that day on, he was just one of the sweetest guys on the planet to me.

One of my friends in Animation saw the mobiles, and told me that I should have an exhibit of them in the Disney library. Like I mentioned earlier, the Studios had a wonderful little library, and sometimes other animators would have little shows in there, showcasing their work. I thought that was a fine idea, and signed up to show off my propellers, some kinetic mobiles, and other various artwork I had done on the side. I had to wait about six weeks for the next open spot, but it was well worth it. I set everything up myself. The library had this nice, long hallway, so I put up a few of my prints in there, including my doper posters.

The doper posters came about because, after working in Animation for a few weeks, I realized that I didn't know much about color. I was working with a pencil all day long, so I thought maybe I should go to night school and learn a little bit about incorporating color into my work.

Well, what I realized in night school was you don't learn color. It comes to you. If you paint or draw and start using color, the more you use it, the more you get used to it. It was kind of interesting to not really learn anything at the school. Like I said before, I learned more from working with the guys in the bullpen than anywhere else.

But one good thing that came out of going to night school was an assignment my teacher made me do. He wanted me to make a Christmas card, but have it look like an old woodblock cut. I went to the library, and I got a book about woodblock cuts to learn just what the hell they were. Inside one of the books was this picture of a wooden Indian that I just absolutely loved. I drew my own copy of this wooden Indian, and hung it up in my office at work for a long time.

After it sat there for a while, I thought maybe I could make some sort of poster out of it, just for fun. I started thinking of things it could possibly advertise. He already had tobacco in the drawing, so I wanted to try something a little different.

I thought he might have smoked marijuana as well. I sat on that idea for a while, thinking maybe it was going a little too far, but eventually decided what the hell, and did it. I made a very jokey poster, featuring a version of that wooden Indian, advertising marijuana.

Some of the other Animation folks would come in and tell me how much they liked it. They would always tell me if I ever had any printed up, they would definitely buy one. Well, after hearing that so many times, I thought maybe it would be a good idea to go to the printer and have some done up.

When I first brought them to the printer, he was a little hesitant because he thought it might have been illegal. I told him it was all done as a joke and I meant no harm by it. Luckily, I was able to convince him I was on the straight and narrow, and he did 500 posters for $60.

Every day after that, during lunch and after work, I'd take an armful of these posters and walk around Toluca Lake, trying to get them sold in all of the little shops on consignment. There was one place in Pasadena, called The Balanize Shop, where the owner took one look at them, and loved them.

"The only problem is," he said, "I can't sell them in here. However, I have a wholesale business. If you come up with a series of these kind of posters, I'll wholesale them for you." I thought that was just a marvelous idea, so I went home and came up with some other posters. I did ones about opium, cocaine candy, heroin airlines…a whole line.

Now, realize again that I wasn't glorifying any of these things. They were all very tongue-in-cheek, and I was just having some fun with them. Those doper posters sold like wildfire, though! I thought they were funny, so I put them into my exhibit for other people to enjoy.

I got a call from the librarian one day and she said, "Walt came in and saw your exhibit today."

"Oh, Jesus," I said. "Did he say anything?"

"Well, he walked down the hallway…"

I started to panic a little bit now. I wasn't sure how Walt would react to those posters!

"…did he see my doper posters?"

"Oh yes!" she said. "In fact, he laughed!"

"He laughed?" I was so happy to hear that. That just shows you how the Old Man accepted anything. He wasn't critical about anything you did, as long as you were doing your best.

The bottom line was, 5 years later, Walt remembered my exhibit when they were looking for more people to work at WED. Ward Kimball brought my name up, and all those propellers popped back into Walt's head. He loved them, and he kept them tucked away up there. They helped me get transferred over, so they really did change my life.

I also learned about a delicious treat during my time in Animation. It may sound weird, but all it consisted of was apple pie and Jack Daniels.

There were about 5 animators that would go out to

One of my doper posters.

IT'S KIND OF A CUTE STORY

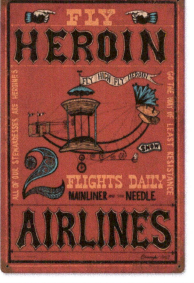

My doper posters.

the desert once or twice during summer to shoot at tin cans. They'd go out with their Stetsons and rifles, and pretend that they were cowboys for a few days. Of course, they would get royally ripped every night.

The one thing they told me they always looked forward to was the apple pie. They would take a spoonful of apple pie, put it in their mouth, and then take a sip of Jack Daniels. They would roll both around in their mouth for a few minutes and then swallow it.

So, of course, I had to try it after that. And let me tell you, it was the most delicious thing I ever did. I still do it today. Try it. Trust me on this, and you'll see how fantastic it tastes. You can thank me later.

Before we get into my move over to WED, I do have to mention the fact that I left Disney for the first time while I was in Animation.

Right after we finished *Lady and the Tramp*, my salary, which was raised up to $70 a week, got cut down to little less than half, to $30. Even with all the jobs on the side that I was doing, there was no way I could support my family with that. I had to leave this amazing job, because the pay just wasn't good enough. In fact, a lot of the guys were going out to try to find other work, and we were just having a terrible time with it.

I heard that milkmen made $100 a week, so I went to a door-to-door milk company to apply. They asked me, "What's your experience?"

"I don't have any!" I told them.

"We can't hire you then. Sorry."

How the hell do you even get experience to be a milkman?

I was off on my own for about 6 months when *The Mickey Mouse Club* started on television. They had all these new animated sequences that needed to be done for the show, so they called me and asked me to come back as an assistant. They started paying my full salary again, and I could support my family while continuing my dream job.

And boy, was I glad I went back.

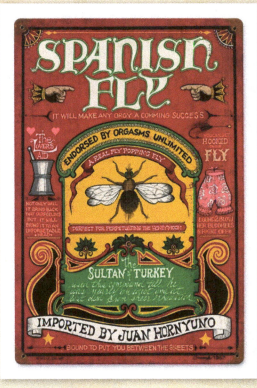

One of my other humorous posters.

CHAPTER 4

DISNEYLAND

efore I get into joining WED, I want to talk a little bit about my thoughts on Disneyland.

Disneyland opened while I was working for Animation. During the last few weeks, right before opening day, they kept pulling guys from Animation to help do last minute things in the Park. Unfortunately, I wasn't one of them, so my first glimpse of the Park wasn't until opening day on July 17th, 1955.

I drove out there with my wife and daughter in my pickup truck. We had a mattress in the bed of the truck, and friends of ours, two other couples, sat on it while we drove to Disneyland. The Park was so damn crowded, you couldn't see a thing. You couldn't even get on any of the rides. I took some 8mm home movies of that opening day, and you can barely see anything in that. I got a lot of shots of the backs of people's heads. I caught glimpses of Debbie Reynolds and Eddie Fisher while shooting footage over the top of a bald guy. It was hot, it was crowded…and I loved every minute of it.

From day one, I've always felt that Disneyland was a gorgeous salad because of the ingredients. There is a little bit of something in there for everyone. The attention to detail is one of the most important pieces of it, because there is so much in there. A good example is the little figures in the popcorn wagons. Those little things are the croutons, or the little bits of oregano, that are in the salad that make it so delicious. I really feel like that was why Disneyland was always so successful. I hate to say it, but the other theme parks were nothing more than just lettuce and tomatoes.

There are a couple of short stories about Disneyland that I want to share, just because I love them.

A lot of people love Main Street, U.S.A. because it hugs them. Walt didn't want to go overboard, so he made them scale everything down when they were building the Park. You feel comfortable as you're walking down the street, because it reminds you of the way things used to be years and years ago. By making you comfortable right off the bat, Walt set the stage for the rest of the Park. He didn't want people to worry about what direction to go in when they got there. You just went down the street, allured by the Castle at the end. Only when you got to the hub did you have to decide what you were going to do next.

I remember hearing a story about Walt wandering around the Park one day, and he really had to go to the bathroom. In those days, there were pay toilets all over the place. It was a pretty common practice to charge to use them, and they cost ten cents. Disneyland had both pay and free toilets in its restrooms. Well, Walt went into the bathroom and noticed that all the free toilets were in use, but the paid ones were completely empty. He checked his pockets, and he didn't have a dime to get into one of the paid ones.

He contacted Maintenance after that, and told them he wanted all of the pay toilets taken out of the Park.

"I don't want any guest to come to Disneyland, and have to go to the bathroom and find it filled!" he said. He wanted people to be able to enjoy everything in the Park. They had already paid to get in; he didn't want them to have to pay to use the restrooms as well. He cared about all the people coming to his Park, and he wanted them to be able to have a good time.

Opposite: **Me in front of Sleeping Beauty Castle in 2008.**

CHAPTER 5

MOVING TO WED

t's a pretty interesting story about how I moved from Animation to WED in 1959. For those of you who don't know, WED Enterprises was the name of the company that was creating everything for Disneyland. WED came from Walt's initials: Walter Elias Disney. Today, people know WED as Walt Disney Imagineering, or WDI.

Anyway, Walt decided that he wanted some more people from the Studio to come over to WED. He already had a few people from Animation that he transferred over, but now the projects were getting larger and he needed more people. Originally, they were working on the studio lot as well, but as they got bigger, he had to move them to a new building.

Walt was holding a meeting one day and said, "You know, we should get some more guys from Animation and get them over there. I need some of your ideas on who would be perfect for that." They're sitting there, thinking, and then Ward Kimball gets an idea.

"Why don't you get Eric Larson's assistant, Rolly Crump?"

Walt's reaction was, "Well, who's Rolly Crump?"

"He's the kid that did all those propellers," Ward told him. Walt liked the propellers a lot, so they decided to try to bring me over. They had someone call Eric Larson, and ask him if it would be okay for me to transfer over to WED.

"No, he's too important in Animation…way too important!" he told them. He really didn't want me to leave. But that was a common problem at the time, though. All the guys in Animation started calling WED 'Cannibal Island,' because it was stealing all these great people from them. People would go off to WED, and never be heard from again by the Animation folks!

So, they relented, and let it pass.

A few weeks later, Walt was having another meeting and brought the same topic up again.

"You know, we still haven't picked anybody else yet to come over to WED."

Ward, again, mentioned my name.

"Well, I tried to get him but Eric told me he was too important to their department," Walt told him.

"He's not too important for Animation, for God's sakes!" Ward replied.

Now, they cut out the middle man, and called me in directly to ask if I wanted to work for WED.

I was already aware of WED before that, obviously. I worked in the model shop with some of the guys out there, so I knew what it was like. I did some little things that were in the movies for WED, such as a backdrop here or there, even though I was still an employee in Animation. I liked what they were doing, and wanted to try something new, so I agreed.

"When can I start?" I asked.

"How about Monday?" he replied.

"I'm there!"

It's kind of funny, because Eric Larson was in Europe on vacation when I abandoned him. I always felt really sorry for that. When Eric came back, I was no longer his assistant but he accepted that. He knew that I was looking for work outside of Disney, because I felt I had pretty much become stagnated being an assistant

Opposite: **Me outside of my art gallery on Ventura Boulevard.**

animator. I didn't see any growth in it, and I didn't want to be an animator forever. I knew that I didn't have the drive or the talent. I needed something else, and WED was the perfect outlet for me.

I ran into him a few years later and said, "God, Eric, I'm sorry for leaving you like that!"

He said, "No, no that was the smartest thing you ever did." So it all worked out well in the end.

The first time I actually met Walt was my first day at WED.

Walt said, "Roland, it's nice to have you aboard."

"Well, thank you, Sir" I replied. "I just want to say, Mr. Disney, that it's a pleasure for me to meet you and be part of this organization."

He got that sparkle in his eye, one I would see many times in the coming years, and said, "Roland, the name is Walt and don't you forget it!"

Speaking of names, there's a cute story about Walt forgetting mine while I was working there. He knew me as Roland when I started at WED, and that's who I was for about a year. But then one day, while sitting in a meeting, he started calling me Owen. I didn't have a clue where that came from, but I didn't say anything. This went on for a while. Turns out, there was a writer, named Owen Crump that was working for the Company as well. He wrote a lot of live action films, so his name was always heard around. Walt must have gotten us confused, and just starting calling me Owen.

Of course, I didn't care what he called me. I was working for Walt Disney, so he could call me whatever he wanted. I'd be Owen, that wasn't a problem!

Then one day, I'm suddenly being called Orland. I still have no idea where that name came from! I talked to Walt's daughter about it one time, and she said that her father had a lot of trouble with names. But again, I didn't mind.

After being Orland for a few weeks, a bunch of us were in a meeting about the Haunted Mansion, when Walt turned to Yale Gracey, one of the other guys working on the project, and said, "Yale I want you and what's-his-name here to work on the Mansion together." Of course, the 'what's-his-name' he was referring to was me.

Soon after, though, Walt gave me the nickname Rolly, and that's what has stayed with me. The interesting thing is that I was called Rolly when I was a little kid, because I'm a junior. My full name is Roland Fargo Crump, Jr. My family used to call me Little Rolly, and now here I was again, being called Rolly by Walt Disney. It kind of brought the name full circle. Bob Gurr and Marty Sklar still call me Orland sometimes, but for everyone else, it was Walt's nickname of Rolly that has stuck.

When I transferred to WED, they didn't know what to do with me at first. They kept giving me little jobs to do here and there, nothing too crazy. I was making puppet hands out of balsa wood for a while. I didn't mind, though, because I was at WED finally. I would have done whatever they wanted.

Then Claude Coats started working on the Wizard of Oz ride. This was supposed to go in Rock Candy Mountain, where the Storybook Land boat ride is now. He came to me and said, "We're going to have this big field in front of Emerald City, and I'd like to have it filled with propellers. Can you do that?" Of course, I said sure and got right to work. I made lots of them for the model, but since the ride was never built, I never built the full scale ones.

I was in some of the meetings with Walt about the Oz ride. Funny thing about Walt was that he loved to act stuff out. One time, he looked at me and said, "I'm going to be the host of the ride, and you're going to be Dorothy." I had to stand up and act the whole thing out with him, how people would be welcomed into their boat and so on. It was a riot.

After that, Walt asked me to do some propellers for the set of the movie *Babes in Toyland*. I had them designed as flowers with faces. Their arms, which were up in the air, were the propellers. I also did a little mobile out of cockleshells. It was funny, though, because I wasn't technically supposed to be working on the live action feature films. I had to sneak around to do some of these jobs on the lot so none of the Union guys would see me. One time, they ran over to me, grabbed a paint brush out of my hand and threw it across the street. I said, "What the hell did you do that for?" But they just motioned over to the Union

Opposite: Match box covers of *Animals Staring*.

IT'S KIND OF A CUTE STORY

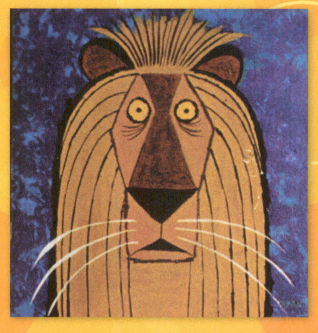

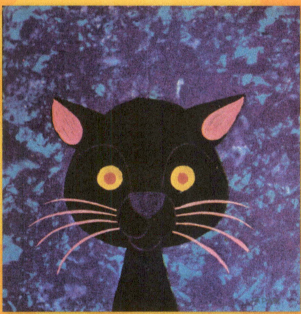

representative who was making his way toward me.

In WED, I had to experience something that I'd never really came in contact with in Animation before: egos. To be clear, there is nothing wrong with having an ego. It's all part of the business. In other words, in order to survive, you kind of had to have an ego, to fight for what you believed in. And I did. A lot!

I was almost 20 years younger than everybody else at WED, so to them I was just a kid from Animation. Sometimes, my things were kind of pushed to the side, but I stood up and defended them every time. I think that's part of the reason why Walt started to like me so much. He would back me in my decisions, and sometimes that didn't sit too well with the other guys.

This would be the first of many times I would be working under Dick Irvine. Dick used to work for 20th Century Fox. He knew how to package things, and how to get them done. There was no denying that he was very good at that. As an administrator, he was incredible. But as an Art Director and a designer, he was a zip. He didn't know a damn thing. And because of that, I used to challenge him a lot which didn't sit too well with him. We used to really go at each other sometimes, but then Walt would step in before it got too crazy to try to smooth things over. We always came to a compromise, but more often than not, it was more in my favor.

I was always honest with Walt, and told him how I really felt about something. Again, I think that's part of the reason why he took such a liking to me. Whenever we had meetings, a lot of the other guys would get up and sing and dance. They were playing the part of the yes man. They'd kind of say what they thought he wanted to hear. If he asked them a question, some of them would start off really strong, and then trail off in a mumble. I knew that Walt knew they didn't know what they were talking about.

But Walt was so faithful to his guys, especially because they did such wonderful work, that he would never call them out on it. However, I promised myself that I wasn't going to be one of those yes men. I was going to be true to myself, and to what I believed in.

It did take me a while to get to that point, though. These meetings would go on for about three years before I was not afraid to really speak my mind. I just watched very carefully how they all acted at first and slowly started to voice my opinion. Then I would voice it a little louder. And then louder still. Eventually, I was the outspoken one.

So, I was a little bit different, and I think Walt liked that about me.

Me kneeling proudly next to some of my work in my art gallery.

During my time at WED, I started talking about selling some of my personal artwork on the side. One of the guys I worked with suggested I open up my own gallery. I thought that was a great idea, so I opened up small one on Ventura Boulevard in Studio City. It took me about a year to put the whole thing together, with all my paintings and posters. My Mom helped run it during the day and I would come in at night to close up shop. Walt actually sent me flowers when I opened up. He'd heard about it through the grapevine, so I thought that was sweet of him to wish me luck like that.

I had some plants inside my gallery to add to the atmosphere. In the evenings, I would take my plants out back to this little area where I could water them. I bent down one night to water them, and I saw two legs and two feet appear in front of me. I wasn't expecting anyone so I wasn't sure who it was.

"Hello?" I asked as I stood up. There was a man standing there with a gun pointed at me and a handkerchief over his face.

Opposite: **More matchbox covers, this time of *Hot Air Balloons.***

Various match box covers I designed.

I said, "Can I help you?"

"Let's go inside," he responded.

We went inside, and I had no idea what to think. He pointed the gun at me and said, "How much money do you have in your wallet?"

"I've only got about $8 in there," I told him.

"Well, where is it?" he asked.

"It's out in my car, out front." That wasn't going to work for him, so he tried again.

"Do you have any other money?"

"Yes, in the cash register." I had one of those old-fashioned cash registers in the back, and had about $45 in there. He wanted to take a look, so we went in the back to get it. The interesting thing about those old cash registers is that you can't just hit a button and they pop open. You had to lift the lid, push a button and then take the contents out. I thought, 'God, I hope he doesn't think there is a gun hidden in there!'

I lifted the lid slowly, and told him exactly what I was doing so he wouldn't get trigger happy. At this point, he and I are having a pretty nice conversation. I mean, here he was trying to rob me, and I'm making conversation with the guy.

The drawer flew open, and he saw the $45 in cash. I gave him that, but he declined to take the loose change. It was about this time I began to wonder how he was going to leave. I wasn't sure if he was going to hit me in the head, or lock me in a closet or something like that before he took off. I must have had a strange look on my face while I was thinking about that because he noticed how distressed I was looking. He thought I was upset about losing the money.

He looked at me and said, "Do you really need this money?"

"Well, yes and no," I told him. "But I think you should have it, though."

It was at this point that we started arguing over who should have the money.

"I'll give it back to you."

IT'S KIND OF A CUTE STORY

Another painting I did.

"No, no, you went through this much trouble to get it, it's yours."

"It seems like you really need it, though, you should take it back."

We went back and forth like this for a minute or two.

Finally, we decided he should keep it.

When he was getting ready to leave, I told him, "You know, I'm going to have to call the police about this."

He said that was fine, but asked that I wait 5 minutes before I left the gallery. I didn't have a phone in there, so I would have to go across the street to use the one at the bowling alley. I assured him I would wait even longer than that, not to worry! I had fully planned on pouring myself a glass of wine before even considering leaving, anyway.

He started going out the back door, $45 in hand, and I called out to him.

"Excuse me, Sir?" I said.

He looked back to me, "Yes?"

"Do me a favor? Don't come back." He left with a chuckle, and thankfully, I never saw him again.

True to my word, I sat there and had a glass of wine before going across the street to report the whole thing to the police.

Local newspaper clipping of the robbery at my art gallery.

Gunman Hesitates, Takes $45

STUDIO CITY — A gunman who held up a small art gallery Monday night almost relented and gave back the $45 loot.

But, police said, he changed his mind again, and remarked "I guess I need it more than you do. You've got an art store and I don't have one," then disappeared in the dark.

Roland Crump, owner of the gallery at 12658 Ventura Blvd., said the dark haired man wore a mask and carried a revolver. No paintings were touched.

CHAPTER 6

The Haunted Mansion

The next thing I knew, they decided to have Yale Gracey and me work together on the concept for the Haunted Mansion.

Well, Yale was just incredible. He was a genius. He was a guy who would sit there and just tinker with toys just to see how they worked. He built scale replica trains, and did all kinds of models in small scale. He had this incredible little mind on how to do this stuff.

We weren't really given too much direction on the project. At the time, they still didn't really know what they wanted it to be, so they just kind of set us loose. This was a lot of fun for the both of us, especially me, because we were getting paid to have fun! We started coming up with all these illusions. For research, we started reading books on ghosts and went to see movies about them. In fact, we took Walt with us once to see *13 Ghosts*, the film by William Castle. Walt just wanted us to be left alone, and he gave us the freedom to do whatever we wanted. We had our own little studio that we just filled with all sorts of crazy stuff.

Roger Broggie ran MAPO at the time. MAPO was short for Manufacturing and Production Organization, which was the department that created a lot of the Audio-Animatronics. Anyway, for some reason, he didn't like us too much. Walt told us to use him to build the effects for us, because that was his job. So, we went over to him and told him what we wanted, and he asked us what our account number was. Well, we didn't have one, nor did we know what he was talking about!

"Well, I can't build this for you if you don't have an account number." And that was that. We didn't tell him that Walt told us to ask him to build it for us. We just kept our mouths shut. We decided to find someone else or just do it ourselves. We enlisted the help of Bob Mattey, who was in charge of special effects for some of the Disney films. He was probably most famous for the squid in *20,000 Leagues Under the Sea*.

One day, Walt and Roger came over to check out some of the stuff we'd done. We showed them off, and Walt was pretty impressed. He looked at us and said, "Roger built this for you?"

Now, we could have ratted him out, and told Walt that Roger refused to help us. But instead, we just said Bob Mattey did it. Roger just kind of froze when we said that, because Walt was kind of upset by that.

"You know, you should be using Roger for this stuff!" Yale and I looked at Roger, but he refused to look us in the eye. Walt looked to Roger and told him to do whatever we wanted him to and he just said, "Yes, Walt," and kept his head down. Of course, we never saw Roger again after that, because he still refused to help us, probably out of pride at that point. But all our effects still turned out pretty good in the end.

We had all these fake heads that we had bought at magic shops, because we were just buying all kinds of things. We decided we were going to build monsters from some of them. We took a pig head that we bought and put a platform for the shoulders underneath it. Now, the shoulders under the head were actually film flame lids and underneath that was a big rat trap. We hung a black cloth down around it and painted bones on him. He was a pretty ugly looking guy, and wound up being about seven feet tall.

Yale set it up so that when he shot it with a prop gun, it would blow apart into a few pieces. We didn't know what we were doing; we were just trying stuff out. But it looked neat, and it was set to reassemble itself to do it all over again. One day Walt came in to see how we were doing. Yale handed the gun over to Walt, and let him shoot the monster. So he did, and he blew up, and the pieces went all over the place. Walt liked it and

Opposite: **Me in front of the Haunted Mansion.**

said, "Yes, pretty fun, but how the hell are we going to use that damn thing?" We didn't have a clue! But he left us alone to just kind of explore and do our own thing.

We also had this skull, with shreds of clothing attached to her, hidden in a hole in the floor. She was rigged inside a compressed chamber, so that when you pushed a button, she shot out into the air. We made it so she would scream at the same time, and it just wound up being a neat little effect. That's another one that ended up in the final attraction, too. When you're up in the attic, and those little heads pop up at you, that is an evolution from that.

It wasn't long after that that we got a call from personnel saying, "The janitors have requested that you leave the lights on when you leave at night. You have a lot of crazy stuff in there." We agreed, but then Yale came up with this great little plan. Those days of practical jokes over in the Animation Department never really left us, so we came up with this idea to mess with the janitors.

My wife made a ghost out of China Silk for us. When you turned a fan on it, it looked like the ghost would rise up and shimmer. We sprayed it with black light paint, so he looked pretty neat. We set him up in the room, then we had the monster guy that blew into pieces set up, too. We had some other guys that had lights in their eyes and moaned. We set them all up in this big elaborate display.

When it was all ready to go, Yale and I rigged the room. He put this invisible beam across the floor right by the door so, when someone walked through it, it would turn off the lights and set all these things off. Whoever walked into the room was going to get the scare of their life. Sure enough, when we came into work the next morning, everything was going off! The monster guy had been blowing up all night long, the ghosts were flying around and everything else was going nuts. But we knew that we got someone because there was a broom lying on the floor. Later that day, we got another call from personnel telling us, "You've got to clean up your own room from now on, because the janitors are never coming back again!"

After that, we started making full scale mock-ups of scenes we thought would be good to include in the attraction. Yale had come up with this incredible idea. He had this statue of Beethoven, which was only a little head. He took a film out of the library of Hans Conried's face saying, "Magic Mirror, who's the fairest one of all?" Yale projected that little piece of footage onto the Beethoven statue, and it looked like the statue had come to life. That was one of the effects that we showed to Walt that he just loved, and it eventually found its way into the Haunted Mansion when it was finally built. You'll recognize it as the effect on the marble busts singing in the graveyard sequence.

We also built a model of the elevator stretch room at about a half-inch scale. We made it out of metal, and so they could see how it worked. That was another one that we got the idea for from an old World's Fair pavilion. People would walk into this building but you'd never see them come out. We thought, 'Gee, what a great idea to have people walk into this Haunted Mansion, and never see where they went…and then you walk in right after them!'

Yale asked me to develop the look for the stretch paintings while he worked out the mechanics of the elevator. I designed about half a dozen different portraits, all just simple pen and ink layouts. Somewhere along the line, Marc Davis heard about them, and came in to look at my sketches. He basically said, "They're no good. I'm going to redo them!" That didn't really bother me because I admired him so much and I thought he'd do a better job than I would anyway.

Yale found out about the famous Pepper's Ghost effect from the book *The Boy Mechanic*. The book shows you how to make things appear and disappear by using reflections on a glass panel. Yale had designed this thing where you would reflect something offstage into the glass, and have it look like it's in the room. We did a full scale mock-up of a scene using that effect.

Originally, a sea captain was going to be part of the story for the Haunted Mansion. He was drowned at sea, but he sometimes would come back to this house to check on things. We made a full scale mock-up of what we thought his study would look like in the Mansion. We had the curtains blowing in the wind, and you could see the ocean off in the distance, with the waves breaking on the shoreline. We had the lonely cry of a coyote in there, too. As you're looking at all this, we had it so the sea captain himself appeared before you. He had a skull for a head, with seaweed hanging all over his yellow rain slicker. We had him offstage under a simulated rain shower, with a big pan of water under him. It looked like water was running all over the floor. It was one hell of an illusion!

When we turned him on, his reflection would hit the glass, and it would look like he was right in the middle of the room we created for him. You'd see the water dripping off him and onto the floor. We turned the light that was over him on real slowly so he would appear real slowly into the room. It made it more ghost like. The story at the time was he had murdered his wife and bricked her up in the fireplace in his study. As he turns and looks around the room, we had the ghost of the murdered bride appear in the wall. All of a sudden, she came screaming toward him with her bony arms, and they both disappeared. It was one of the best illusions that we ever came up with, I thought. The problem was they couldn't use it in the Mansion!

When we first started working on all these things, it was a walkthrough attraction. Not only that, but there were supposed to be two Mansions, not just one. That way, even as a walkthrough, Disney would get the hourly capacity that wanted. That's why there are two stretch rooms to begin with, because they each would have gone off to their own separate Mansion. Of course, the guests would have never known any different.

Anyway, you would have walked from room to room. You'd be in each room for at least three minutes, so we staged all these great little gags that you would see. The sea captain room specifically, you had to be standing there, in the same spot, for a few minutes in order for it to work correctly. Unfortunately, they changed it over to a ride like it is today, so that whole idea got squashed.

I think the attraction would have been ten times better if it was kept as a walk through. Operations panicked, though. Disney thought that people would be running loose if it was a walkthrough, and God only knew what they might do. They didn't think anyone would know which way to go, and we would need people inside to kind of guide them along.

Yale and I thought we had solved a problem using something we had seen in one of the pavilions at the Seattle World's Fair. They had this room where you got off of an elevator and you walked into this great big area that was pitch black. All of a sudden, down a little ways, a light turned on, and people would walk toward it. Then when everybody got there, they just turned that light out, and then turned another one on down a little ways more. People would just automatically go over to where the lights were. They moved about 100 people at a time without anyone telling them where to go!

As kind of a take-off from this, we also thought of having a guide bring you through the Mansion. You'd start at one end of the hallway, and the lights would go out. Then, all the way at the other end, you'd see this ectoplasm floating on the other side of a gate. Eventually, a person would slowly appear there, out of this ectoplasm. That person would become the Ghost Host who would take you on the tour. The reason for that gate was because it hid the piece of glass that would create the Pepper's Ghost illusion for the ectoplasm. But Operations thought that kids might do something, and it would take too much security. So that's when they decided to make it a ride.

Really, all of our ideas were out there, but we had so much fun. I never really believed in the supernatural, but Yale did. He told me a great story that he used as inspiration for a lot of his work on the Mansion.

When he was 8 years old, he went to visit relatives on the East Coast. They lived in this big, old house, and Yale spent the summer there with his cousins. When it came time to go home, his Mom asked him what he enjoyed most about his visit, and he said, "The little old lady that lives in the closet and reads to us every night."

All of his cousins were yelling, "No, no, don't tell them, she'll never come back!" But Yale's Mom and aunt were very concerned. They had no idea what he was talking about. His aunt eventually did some research on the house, and found a photo of the people that lived there before them. When she showed it to her kids, they said one of the people in the photo was the same woman who used to read to them at night. But after Yale told his Mom about it, the ghost of that woman never came back. Yale was about as straight as they came, and never told a lie, so I knew he really had that experience. It was incredible.

I think out of everything Yale and I designed together, only about 25% made it into the final attraction. That was mostly because of the change to the storyline, and the fact that the Mansion was changed into a ride rather than a walk through. You have to remember that this was the first attraction to be designed without Walt's full guidance. Unfortunately, he passed away before any final decisions about it could be made, so it turned into sort of a mess. I think it is fine the way it is now, but it could have been so much better. Walt always wanted it as a walkthrough, and I think it would have worked out better if they'd stuck to his original vision.

CHAPTER 7

ADVENTURELAND BAZAAR

n 1961, Walt moved WED from the Disney studio lot over to Sonora Street in Glendale to another, smaller building. Believe it or not, there were only 60 of us in that new building at the time, and that included all the secretaries and everyone else. It was amazing what this small group of people managed to produce. I would think as far as designers went, there wasn't more than eight of us altogether. It was amazing, because with just the eight of us, we were going to tackle all these upcoming projects for Disneyland, as well as for the World's Fair.

When we first moved over there, Dick Irvine said to me, "We're going to give you a chance at being an Art Director." I was kind of surprised by this, but gladly accepted the position.

There was an area in Adventureland with a little shop called the Bazaar. You may know it today as this nice breezy looking place, but back when the Park first opened, Adventureland Bazaar was real dark, and it looked like it was just thrown together over a weekend.

So Dick said, "I want you to get in there and redo it. Make it so that it makes some money!" Because, at the time, nobody was going in there to buy their rubber lizards. So I accepted the challenge.

In those days, I believe Dick was still very closely connected with Grosh Studios, because they used to build all the scenic drops for MGM and 20th Century Fox Studios, where Dick had come from. So, he wanted to continue using them, and put them on as the contractor for this project. WED was very different back then. We didn't have any of those in-house capabilities that they have now, like carpentry or any of that technical stuff. We were just a design studio and that was that.

We had our meeting with Grosh, and told them what we had to do. We gave them the square footage of the room we were going to do it in, and they gave us a price. The next thing I know, I was shipped down to a sound stage at Allied Studios, where we had rented some space. Then the real challenge was presented before me. I had to put this damn thing together and I had just six weeks to do it in with no drawings, plans, or anything! Everything had to be done from scratch.

Luckily, I was working closely with Jack Olsen, who was the head of Merchandise at the time. Jack fancied himself as being an interior designer, because he'd done all the shops at Disneyland, mostly on his own. He was great designer, and he knew what he was doing, so I was glad to have his help.

I met with Jack about the project, after I got the price from Grosh for what it would cost. Jack listened to me as I relayed what they said, but then this little light bulb seemed to go off above his head.

"You know, Rolly we should go to the boneyard," he said.

I just kind of looked at him and said, "What the hell is the boneyard?" He smiled a bit at that. "Well," he replied, "We have a lot of stuff at Disneyland. But every once in a while, something becomes worn out or broken down. Then we have to build something new to take its place. Everything that we've replaced in the past five years, we never threw out. We put it in the boneyard."

I was pretty curious about that, because I'd never heard of it before. I asked him what kind of goodies they had there.

Opposite top: The entrance to Adventureland Bazaar.
Opposite bottom: Interior of Adventureland Bazaar. On the left is one of the old Disneyland ticket booths that I converted into a display stand and register station.

Interior of Adventureland Bazaar.

"Pretty much anything you can think of," he said. "Like the old tickets booths." When the Park first opened, you bought your general admission entry, and then you bought tickets for the different rides. That's where the A, B, C, D and E tickets came from. If you ever ran out while you were in the Park, you could go up to a ticket booth and buy more. They were all over the place.

So we went to the boneyard, and I found these old ticket booths. They were still in pretty good condition, so I decided to use them as cash register stations in the Bazaar. We found a lot of other good stuff there, like streetlights and crates, and we had them shipped back to the sound stage to begin work. I also started sketching different aspects and design elements that I wanted to be in the Bazaar. These were all things that you couldn't just buy off the shelf, and had to be built from scratch. But we also did a lot of things with stuff we could buy, and just designed them differently. I went downtown to buy all sorts of random material, and brought them back to the studio. I would design the patterns that I painted on them, and then I'd help the painters paint them.

Since the Bazaar was kind of in a small area, Jack Olsen gave me this great idea about how to make it seem a little bigger. He told me to use mirrors on the walls. It was just this simple little idea, but it just worked wonders. We used as many mirrors as we could, because all the reflections made it look like it was a lot bigger.

We also had these columns that I salvaged from the boneyard. Now, these columns are what I used to make the entrance of the changing rooms. I just thought it looked neat. The columns used to be from the Chicken Plantation restaurant, I believe. I thought it was so great to take things out of the boneyard, which were essentially being put out to pasture, and then reusing them in our building. I always used to say we really were building the 'Bazaar,' because it was made out of anything we could find, so it really was 'bizarre!'

A great little story from when we were building all this stuff was about my sketches. Again, I didn't have any formal training, so I was just kind of doing it. My work desk was literally an apple box! I'm doing

Interior of Adventureland Bazaar.

these sketches, and I'm giving them to the carpenters. One of the carpenters came up to me and said, "I got your sketches, Rolly, but what's the scale on them?"

I looked at him and said, "Scale? What's scale?"

"Well, do you have a scale ruler?" he asked.

"What's a scale ruler?" I replied. I didn't have a clue!

He took one of my drawings and said, "Well, let's work through this."

We're looking at my drawing, and I'm going, "Well, this is about 8 feet tall, and this is about 6 feet…" We made two special little cardboard scale rulers for my sketches: one for me, and one for him. It wasn't standard on mine, obviously. We had it so one and a quarter inch equaled a foot, or something like that. So I got used to using a scale ruler for my work. When I went back to WED one day I asked the guys there to tell me

Interior of Adventureland Bazaar, with a different type of Disneyland ticket booth that I made into a register station.

all about a real scale ruler. They did, but I said, "Eh, I like my little cardboard one better!" At the end of the project, the carpenter stuck his head in my office, showed me our special scale ruler and said, "If we ever work together again, I'll be all ready for you!"

Anyway, back to the Bazaar itself. The interesting thing about it was that I worked seven days a week for six weeks straight to get this thing done. I was working my ass off! However, Dick Irvine didn't think I'd get it done on time. So, he purposely gave me the wrong end date. He gave me a week's lead time, because he assumed I wouldn't get it done on time, and would need that extra week before the real opening date.

So, he told me they were going to open up the Bazaar on a Wednesday, and he gave me the date. I thought to myself, 'Okay, fine. I can do this.' It was my responsibility to get everything shipped there from Grosh Studios the weekend before. I would have to get it all installed by at least Monday or Tuesday so the electricians could get in there and get their work done. It was all planned out in my mind, and I was ready to go.

Every Friday, I had to check in with Dick to give him my progress report on how things were going. Well, when I went to him that Friday right before the final deadline, I told him I was right on time with the schedule he had given me. Of course, he wasn't expecting me to say that. Like I said, he had lied to me about the due date. I was actually a week *early*, but he didn't tell me that. He didn't want to admit he lied.

Me, leaning against one of the old, converted ticket booths, in Adventureland Bazaar, a few days after the shop opened.

Funny enough, I found out about his lies through the grapevine right before that meeting. I kept that to myself, though, and decided I would really stick it to him. So I went to him and said, "We're packing everything up, and taking it to Disney tomorrow. Are you guys ready for us?"

He started to panic a little bit, but still, he didn't want me to know that he'd lied. He was trying to keep his cool, but I could tell he was losing it a little bit.

"Let me check and see how the things are at the Bazaar..." he said. Silently, he was praying that they would be ready. He called Joe Fowler, who was in charge of Disneyland at that time, and told him that we were coming down the next day to install everything.

"But the floor isn't in yet," Joe replied.

Dick was surprised by that. He couldn't believe it! So Dick asked him to repeat that.

"The floor is not in. There is no floor in the place yet!" Joe told him again. Now Dick was REALLY starting to panic.

"Well, you better get the floor in, because we're shipping that stuff down tomorrow!" Dick still refused to back down and just say, "Rolly, you know what? I lied to you." No, he didn't want to do that. He was too proud. Meanwhile, I'm kind of giggling about it to myself, watching him run around, freaking out like that. It was my own silent victory. They had the guys work all night long to put the floor in and finish up the additional touches. I felt bad about that, but I was sticking to my guns on that one! Thankfully, it was all done in time, and we got in there to install it.

Despite being done way ahead of schedule, we didn't open the store until about two weeks later. It was on one of those Grad Nites, where high schools bring their graduating classes in to spend a night in the Park, so all the local kids were there.

I remember that, earlier that afternoon, two nice ladies came into the Bazaar carrying hats, rubber lizards, rubber snakes and such in boxes.

"Can we put our hats and lizards in here?" they asked me.

IT'S KIND OF A CUTE STORY

The hat shop, across the way from Adventureland Bazaar, which was built in just a few hours.

"Sure," I told them. "Are you going to sell them out of the Bazaar?"

"No, no, no," one of them replied. "We're selling them out of our hat shop out there." They pointed over by the Jungle Cruise.

I looked out to see where they were pointing, but there was nothing there!

"What hat shop?" I asked, awfully confused.

"Oh, it'll be there this afternoon…"

I kept looking at that empty space, thinking that maybe they were going to bring a cart or something in to use as their shop. In any event, Grad Nite was going to start at 7 PM, so I had to worry about getting my store ready for business.

Funny enough, around 3:30 PM, some carpenters showed up. Then the electricians. Then the artistic guys. It was almost like looking at time-lapse photography with all these people showing up. In three hours, they built this damn hat shop.

I was amazed! You wouldn't get something done like that today. It would take months just to draw up the plans and engineering, and then weeks to get everything approved. You'd be lucky if something was up in 3 months, let alone 3 hours. That just shows you what a different environment Disney was back then.

That night was the first time Walt saw the Bazaar. He came in to talk to me for a while, and kind of explore the store. He loved the mirror idea, so I have to thank Jack Olsen for that. Walt came in with Lilly, and that was the first time I met her. I was pretty grungy at that point, though. I had been working for days doing these last minute adjustments. I had on this big old straw hat and I hadn't shaved in a couple of days. I looked kind of like a mess.

But Walt came up to me, and shook my hand and said, "Rolly, you did great." He turned to his wife and said, "I want you to meet my wife Lilly. Lilly, this is Rolly." I held my hand out and she got a little look on her face, like, 'Oh God, do I have to shake this kid's hand?' But she was very gracious, kind, and a sweetheart.

Walt pointed her toward one of the mirrors and said, "Look at the shop, Lilly! It goes on, and on, and on!" She kind of looked at him and laughed. He was like a little kid at times, and he just loved seeing all of it for the first time. I loved seeing him like that, especially when it was because of something I had done, so I was very happy about that. It was a pretty special moment for me.

CHAPTER 8

The Enchanted Tiki Room

he Enchanted Tiki Room will always have a special place in my heart. It is an attraction that really deserves a lot of credit, because it was the first all animatronic show that was ever designed and built anywhere in the world. It was a first for Disneyland and a first for the rest of the world, so that is a pretty big deal.

I'm sure most of you know the story by now, but originally Walt wanted a tea room on Main Street where people could come in, have some tea, and see a little show while they ate. Eventually it evolved beyond that, and it was decided that it would be moved over to Adventureland, since they were re-designing it, and turned into a Tiki Room. People would come in for dinner and see this magical little show.

There was this concept sketch that John Hench, one of the leading Art Directors, drew of what he thought The Tiki Room should look like. It was a beautiful drawing, with all these birds sitting over the tables in their cages, chirping down to the people eating. We had our first meeting with Walt about it, and John showed it off because he was very proud of it. Walt turned to John and said, "We can't have birds in there!"

John was a little amazed, and said, "Well, why not?"

"Because they will poop on the food," Walt said matter-of-factly.

John looked back to him and said, "No, Walt they're not going to be real birds. They're going to be fake birds . . . stuffed birds."

Walt was a little put off by the idea, and said, "Disney doesn't stuff birds and put them in a restaurant!" It was interesting to watch these two men, because there was this dialogue going on where John was very adamant about his idea but was backpedaling a bit to make it what Walt wanted.

So John says, "No, no Walt. They just look stuffed. They are little mechanical birds."

"Oh, they're little mechanical birds, eh?" Walt replied.

There was a whole group of us in the room during that meeting, and one of the other guys, I forget who, said, "Well, yeah, you know, we could have birds all over the place so they would surround the people eating. You could sit in the restaurant and listen to these birds chirp to each other."

Walt got that sly smile across his face and said, "Oh, we're going to have birds chirp to each other. I see." You can tell he was really starting to like the idea, and how it was evolving. That was part of the beauty of these sessions. Ideas would come out, and just flow and evolve into these wonderful things that would eventually make their way into Disneyland.

Out of that first meeting, we were all assigned to do different things to try to get this restaurant off the ground. Walt came up to me and said, "Rolly, we're going to have this preshow area for people who are waiting to get into the restaurant. I want to have some Tikis out there, and I want them to tell stories. I want you to design them." I had no choice but to say okay to him, but I didn't know a damn thing about Tikis! I had no idea what I was going to do.

Luckily, John Hench was a good friend of mine, so I went to him and said, "What the hell do I do?"

"Well," he said, "The best thing you can do is some research. Go get a book out of the library about the Gods of the Pacific."

So, off I went to the library. I found this book called *Voices on the Wind*, which was written by Katharine

Opposite: Maui, in place and ready to go.

The Midnight Dancer, in place at the Enchanted Tiki Room.

Luomala, a missionary that lived with the Islanders for a while to learn their customs and their history. She wrote down all the myths and legends that they had, and it was incredibly interesting. The book became a bible for me during the project because it was just so full of information. I was able to reach into these stories and do some sketches of what some of the Tikis might look like, and the stories behind them.

The first one I designed was, funny enough, not a real Tiki. If you've been to Disneyland before, you'll recognize it as the Tiki God spitting water into a piece of bamboo. When the bamboo fills up, it dumps the water down below it, and swings back up to hit a log between its legs behind it. It makes this neat little noise. The Japanese use similar things in their gardens to keep the rabbits and the deer away. Anyway, I drew that concept up, and I was very proud of that one. But remember that it wasn't a real Tiki God, so I didn't give it a name. That'll come into play later on.

The next one I did was Hina, who was the Goddess of mist and rain. I designed it so the water would come out from underneath the brim of her hat, surrounding her, sort of like a backwards umbrella. We also had Pele, who was the Goddess of volcanoes and fire. We added little flames that would shoot out of her, which kind of surprises some folks when it happens.

I showed all these and a bunch more to Walt, and he seemed to enjoy them. He looked at the one I did without a name, and goes, "Tell me…that one doesn't have a title. What's this one do?"

I didn't know what to say! I didn't think he was going to ask specifics about them, so I just kind of kept putting off naming that one. Well, thankfully Hench was standing there at the time. Because of the bamboo thing filling with water and then dumping itself out, Hench stepped up real quickly and said, "It's the God of Tapa cloth beating." But Walt mistook the word 'cloth' for 'clock.'

So Walt just kind of looked at it, and said, "Clock?"

Not missing a beat, John shook his head and said, "It's the God that tells the time."

Walt smiled and shook his head okay to approve it, and we moved on. When the meeting was over, John turned to me and said, "You better go back to your book and find out who the God that tells time is!" I ran back to the book to look it up, and it turns out the name was Maui. That was just another one of those happy accidents that worked out well in the end.

Walt approved all the designs, so then it came time to sculpt them. It's kind of a cute story, because as soon as Walt bought off on them, I went to the head sculptor at the time, Blaine Gibson, and told him that he needed to get started on them as soon as he could.

Blaine just kind of looked at them and said, "I don't have time!"

"Well, then, who's going to sculpt them?" I asked.

IT'S KIND OF A CUTE STORY

He looked at me and said, "You are!"

I said, "I am?"

I'd never sculpted before in my life, so Blaine had to give me a real down and dirty lesson on how to do it. He told me how to build the armatures, which hold the sculpt itself, and how to put the clay on it.

We used plasticine clay to sculpt them out of, and if you don't know, when it's cold, plasticine clay is very hard. You have to get it warmed up to get it real soft to be able to use. That way, when you build an armature, you have the clay soft enough to press it into the armature. Well, it was too cold in the building to be sculpting with plasticine. So, I put the Tiki armatures on wheels, and took them into the parking lot where the sun was shining, so it would be nice and warm. I sculpted the Tikis right there in the parking lot! You may think that people that are sculpting for Disney have got these gorgeous temperature controlled rooms, filled with North light, to better aid their work. But no, no…they have a parking lot! I always thought that was kind of funny.

It gets even better. You know what I sculpted with? A plastic fork! One I got right out of the Studio's cafeteria. I would get the clay on the armature, and then would use the fork to scrape it like it was cut with a knife or bamboo. Like I said before, I had never sculpted before in my entire life before that, so I think I did a pretty good job of it. The first piece I ever sculpted was Maui, the infamous, formerly unnamed, teller of time.

Sketch of Maui, the God of telling time (redrawn from original).

There's a great little story about that Maui statue, actually. It goes back to when I was still researching these Tiki Gods, so I could be as authentic as possible with their representations. In the islands of the Pacific, at certain times of the afternoon, just as the sun is getting ready to set, you can see seven rays that come down from it. Legend has it that those seven rays are ropes that the Gods put around the sun to control it. Before that, the sun used to set whenever it wanted to, putting time all out of whack.

Maui, being the God of time, decided to put a stop to this. He lassoed those ropes around the sun, so if the sun set too soon, he'd just jerk it right back up again. That's why, on the statue in the Enchanted Tiki Room, we have a sun with ropes around him.

Once the Tikis were all sculpted, they were sent over to the Studio where molds were made out of them. They took the molds, and cast them in fiberglass so they would last out in front of the attraction. After that, they sent them back to us at WED. I ended up painting them myself. When I was finished, I had them shipped to Disneyland, where I helped bolt them to the ground. That was what was so great about the Company back then. Everything was hands-on at all times, from start to finish.

There is a little side story here. When I was sculpting the Tiki Gods, I'd ride my motorcycle during lunch. One day, when lunch was over and I was parking it, one of the secretaries walked over and told me she'd never ridden on a motorcycle before.

"Get on the back!" I told her. She obliged, and we went for a little ride for a few minutes until she tapped my shoulder and said she had to get back to work. I asked her where her desk was, and told her I would drop her off.

And that's exactly what I did. I rode my motorcycle through the building, and dropped her off right in front of her desk!

It turned out her desk was near Dick Irvine's office. Obviously, he heard the motorcycle engine from

Another shot of Maui.

down the hallway. He opened his door to see what all the racket was and saw the secretary hopping off the back of my motorcycle.

"Oh, it's just Rolly," he said, and shut his door. I rode out the same way I'd come in.

When I was finished with the Tiki Gods, Walt came to me and said, "I want you to design a bird mobile that comes out of the ceiling, with about 100 birds on it. Can you do that for me?"

I said sure, and started doing some sketches on what I thought it should look like.

I quickly found out that there would be no way to put 100 birds on that thing. The system we would be using to lower the mobile into the room and power all the birds ran off of compressed air. There wouldn't be enough room for all those power lines in the mobile itself, so I had to cut it back to about 30 birds. It turned out just fine, though.

I made the birds into showgirls. I designed them with white feathers, and added little sequins to their breasts, so when the whole Tiki Room lit up, they would sparkle. I managed to put a little touch of Las Vegas on those girls. Come to think of it, I sculpted a good portion of the Tiki Room, too!

I had to install that mobile, too. They sent me up on a lift because I needed to work 15 feet up in the air to get it functioning properly. They let me down only when I had to go to the bathroom or when I wanted lunch. That was kind of fun doing that!

Once we got the room finished, and started testing everything, I took a careful look around. I really liked it, except for the drummers up on the walls, beating their drums. They looked just a little bit dull, and that really bothered me. I tried to think of a way to liven them up a bit, and, of course, the answer was one of the simplest solutions I could think of. I took little sparkles, like we'd used on some dark rides, climbed up and screwed them into their eyes.

When they beat their drums, these sparkles would move and start flickering due to the vibrations. It looked like their eyes were twinkling. It did wonders, and really enhanced the whole show, in my opinion.

It was after that, as we were running it through its paces back at WED, that Walt decided it was going

IT'S KIND OF A CUTE STORY

The Tiki drummers that I put sparkles in the eyes of.

to be a show instead of a restaurant. He thought that no one would want to leave the restaurant while all this was going on around them. We made some simple adjustments, and made a show out of it. We had already ordered all of these tables and chairs to put in the restaurant, so we just moved the tables to another location, and set the chairs up around the fountain in the center. They used those chairs for almost 40 years before someone realized that replacing them with benches would increase the hourly capacity of the show.

I think it's worth mentioning the wonderful rain effect that Yale Gracey had come up with. He used strips of Mylar, cut into really thin ribbons. They were all attached to a little motor at the top, so when it vibrated, it looked like it was raining. It was a magnificent little effect that was so simple, yet so effec-

tive. When they built the attraction at Walt Disney World, someone had the bright idea of using real water instead of Mylar. They spent all this money creating this water system, and it just looked terrible. The real water didn't look like rain at all! The water didn't have the shimmer to it like the Mylar did, so they eventually tore out that expensive system, and replaced it with the cheap Mylar effect, and it looked beautiful again.

When it opened at the Park, it was the only attraction at Disneyland that you had to pay extra for. United Airlines was the sponsor of it back then, and they wanted to charge a little extra for it. They made you pay a dollar to go see it, but it didn't seem to bother the public so much because the show was so beautiful.

We all had a great time working on it, and Walt loved the Tiki Room. It was one of the most popular attractions back then, and still is today. It's great to see how timeless it has become.

Me about to put some final touches on Maui before the Enchanted Tiki Room opens.

CHAPTER 9

THE 1964-1965 NEW YORK WORLD'S FAIR

 Back in the early 1960s, we were working on the World's Fair projects that Walt had picked up. We started with just the Ford pavilion, then added the General Electric one, and finally we were contracted by the state of Illinois to work on Great Moments with Mr. Lincoln. So, we already had these three pavilions to do, which was going to be a lot of work. I was working on an assignment for Ford's Magic Skyway at that time. Walt felt people in the queue needed something to look at and listen to, so he asked me to design a mechanical orchestra.

I did a whole series of sketches of crazy little instruments, which almost had a Rube Goldberg quality to them. Walt took one look and said, "Maybe you should make them look like they're car parts, being the Ford pavilion and all."

Well, obviously, that was a great idea. I can't believe I didn't think of that. I went to Bob Gurr, who was the mechanical genius at WED at the time. The two of us sat down and went through a catalog of Ford

The orchestra made up of car parts that I designed for the Ford Pavilion.
Opposite: Me in front of my iconic creation, the Tower of the Four Winds.

car parts. We picked out some random ones that I thought I could make look like musical instruments. You know, we'd take an axle and cut it in half. Then we'd add part of a carburetor to it, weld a pulley onto one end, and voilà…it looked like a trumpet. When it all came together, I thought it looked pretty damn good.

There is another cute little story about the Ford pavilion. Blaine Gibson was working on the attraction itself, particularly the cavemen and women for the Primeval World sequence. They had just finished a life sized fiberglass model of this Cave Girl, and he was checking her out. She had rubber skin, a wig and a piece of fur around her waist. Other than that, she was stark naked.

Her rubber skin was already painted, but Blaine wasn't sure it was the right color. He wanted to compare it with a real person's skin. He asked me to come over, take off my shirt, and stand next to her. I thought he was joking at first, but he wasn't, so I thought why the hell not. I took off my shirt and shoes, and rolled up my pant legs to really get into the role.

Now you have to imagine how they modeled this Cave Girl. She was a large girl. And by large, I mean both in terms of height and endowment. And there was nothing hiding her endowments!

So I got up next to her, and wrapped myself in some fur to match her.

Blaine started taking some photos with a Polaroid camera. After a few shots, I decided to have some fun with the whole thing. I grabbed that Cave Girl here, there, everywhere! It was entirely immature, but it was funny to me. Besides, Blaine kept right on taking shots. When he was done, he thanked me and we got back to work. By the next day, I had forgotten all about it.

About two weeks later, Walt came over for a meeting and asked Blaine about something. I'm not entirely sure what it was, but Blaine thought the answer might be in one of the many Polaroids he kept in a file.

And that's when I remembered what I did two weeks before. And now Blaine was going through all his Polaroids, with Walt looking over his shoulder. I was in big trouble.

Suddenly, I heard Walt say, "What's THAT?" I knew exactly what he was looking at.

Blaine remained calm and told Walt that he'd asked me to pose with the Cave Girl so he could check her skin value.

Walt looked right at him and said, "I want to see those."

As Blaine put all the shots of me having my way with the Cave Girl on a table for Walt to examine, I stood up to excuse myself. I walked over to the soda machine because my stomach was doing flips. I thought I was about to lose my job. As I walked away, though, I heard Walt laughing.

I got a drink, and started to sip it nervously. A few minutes later, Malcolm Cobb, a friend of mine, came over to check on me. He wasn't part of the meeting, but he saw me walk away, so he wanted to make sure I was okay, especially because I was as white as a ghost.

"Walt's looking at those pictures of me and the Cave Girl," I told him.

His eyes got wide.

"What did Walt think of them?" he asked me.

"Well, I think he laughed," I said.

Just then, I felt someone behind me, and turned around to see Walt standing there.

"You're damned right he laughed, Roland!" Walt said. With that, he turned and walked away.

Nowadays, if I pulled that kind of thing at WED, I'm not sure what would happen to me. Luckily, Walt realized my sense of humor and that I was a little crazy around the edges. He took it in stride, and that helped cement our working relationship.

One day, not too long after that, there was an emergency meeting called. Walt came in and he said to us, "Well, there is one more piece of real estate left at the World's Fair. I'd like for us to get it." We all looked around at each other in disbelief. Did he really just say what we thought he said? Apparently, Pepsi-Cola wanted to be the sponsor, and it would be a salute to UNICEF.

"I'd like to do a little boat ride," he continued. Well, we all kind of thought to ourselves, 'Oh my God, he's lost it.' Our plates were already full. We had to perfect the show for Mr. Lincoln, the first time in history that an animatronic figure was going to stand up. We were working on Carousel of Progress for General

The Tower of the Four Winds, in front of It's A Small World on a slow day at the World's Fair.

IT'S KIND OF A CUTE STORY

The Tower of the Four Winds in its heyday.

IT'S KIND OF A CUTE STORY

Electric's Progressland, with all the animatronics that were going in there. We had to make sure the conveyance system worked for the Ford pavilion. And here he was, wanting to do a little boat ride, too!

So, that first meeting was kind of odd, because we didn't know how to react. But Walt wanted it, so Walt was going to get it! So, of course, what everyone actually said was, "Sure, Walt, sure!" That was the beginning of It's A Small World.

As you can imagine, things started to move very rapidly at that point. Walt came to me and said, "Rolly, I'm going to need a marquee for the front of this thing." So he gave me the task of designing the Tower of the Four Winds. What I loved about that was when he explained what he wanted, it was basically a tower of mobiles. That meant Walt had remembered the propellers I had designed way back when, so that was really special to me. That was just the way his mind worked. He remembered things that you did, and just sort of tucked them away in the back of his head to use later.

I got to work, and produced a sketch of an elaborate design. Walt liked it, and asked me to build a model of it.

It wasn't until then that I realized that it was going to be a structure. I had to start thinking about it in a different way. If it was going to be a structure, I thought, I had better put some arches in it for support, like the Eiffel Tower has. Those arches wound up being the base of it.

I started attaching vertical pieces to the arches. I wasn't an engineer, but I was trying to think like one. I didn't want everything to be freestanding but all connected together somehow. If this piece moved, then it caused that piece to move, and so on, all working together to create movement.

I showed that model to Walt, and he liked it a lot, so we sent it off to be built full-size. The model and the plans were shipped off to the Kelite Corporation, who were going to build it. They assembled it for us to inspect before shipping it off to New York.

When they had finished building it for us, Walt asked me to drive him over to their yard to check it out. Can you imagine driving Walt Disney someplace? It was just a trip.

"Alright, Rolly," he said to me. "Put on your seat belt, and let's go." I hardly ever wore a seat belt at the time, but I wasn't going to disobey the boss. Not even in my own car!

To be honest, I was originally pretty put off by the Tower's construction. My nice little design looked quite crazy when it was built to withstand hurricane force winds and scaled up to full size. The little 6 inch diameter pipes I designed became 12 inch so it could hold itself up. I wasn't too happy with it.

If Kelite had called me and said, "You know, we're going to have to make some of these pipes thicker in order to support the structure, is that okay?", I would have gone back to the drawing board with it. I would have had sessions with them to try to make it work better. I would have made better connections, and maybe added some spider web designs to double as additional support. But they didn't work that way, they just went and did what they were told. I was a little upset by that.

When Walt and I viewed the finished product before shipment, Walt turned to ask me, "Well, Rolly, what do you think?"

I was always honest with Walt, and I think he respected me a little more because of that. Some of the other guys would just 'yes' him to death, but I always told him how I actually felt.

So I said to him, "I hate to tell you, Walt, but I think it's a piece of crap."

Walt looked at me and came back with, "No, no Roland, this cost me $200,000. It cannot be a piece of crap!" He understood where I was coming from, but he'd made his point, so that was that. The Tower of the Four Winds was disassembled and shipped off to New York.

Around the same time, my 'beloved' leader at the time, Dick Irvine, asked Marc Davis to do a sketch of what he thought the inside of Small World would look like. Walt said it was going to be for the 'children of the world,' so it had to fit in that mentality. So, about a week later, Marc brought in this beautiful rendering of what he thought it should look like. Walt took one look at it and said, "What's Mary Blair doing?"

Now, it wasn't a dig against Marc's work or anything. It just wasn't what Walt had in mind. Walt never said no to anybody. He was better at saying, "That's good, but how about we try it this way instead and see what we come up with?"

The reason Walt asked about Mary was because she had a childlike quality in her art. In fact, she had left Disney a few years earlier, and was illustrating for Golden Books, doing a lot of the pictures inside their children's books. They were just gorgeous, too. Dick Irvine put in a call to Mary to see if she'd be interested in this new idea. Of course, she said she'd love to be involved.

Well, that was good news for me. As far as I was concerned, she was a hero to me. I grew up with her work, and as a little kid, saw her a lot on TV in those behind-the-scenes segments with Walt. I always wondered who that little blonde lady was. Then when I was working in Animation, I heard all kinds of stories about Mary, so I really knew quite a bit about her before I met her. She was kind of a Goddess to me. I was thrilled to death when Walt decided to bring her in to do the styling for Small World. I thought, 'Oh my God, I'm going to meet Mary Blair.' She was one of my idols, and I was going to get to work with her.

It was really kind of cute how I first met her. I was sitting in the model shop on top of a step ladder when she came in. She looked up at me and just kind of smiled. She later told me, after I got to know her better, "You were really cute sitting up on top of that step ladder." I thought that was sweet of her.

Working with Mary Blair on It's A Small World for the World's Fair.

When she started, she immediately started doing collage paintings of what the different parts of Small World would look like. Amazingly, I've got a whole book of them still. I had all of her artwork photographed and put into the Archives back then, but I kept copies to make into a little book.

She also did some sketches with Marc Davis that showed some toys on the ride, and they were just wonderful. I loved them. Luckily, I was assigned to design and build the toys for the whole attraction. I started off by myself, but I got really deep into it. Eventually, about 30 people wound up working for me. We had a whole bunch of toys to make. I think we had over 200 toys that we built from scratch. We made them out of Styrofoam and paper-mache. Since Mary's last job was doing those children's books, we went out and bought a few of them to kind of keep the toys in her style. I really thought that was the best way to make sure the toys captured Mary's shapes and feeling.

Kind of as a tribute to her, we slipped one toy doll with short blonde hair wearing Mary's favorite outfit into the ride as a tribute to her. Even though we moved the whole thing over to Disneyland when the World's Fair was over, we still kept it in there. You can still see it today when you visit Disneyland, hanging out on the Eiffel Tower.

Meanwhile, the guys over in the model shop started taking Mary's sketches and developing them into little sets to put into the ride. The interesting thing about it was that Mary didn't know how to interpret her artwork. When they put her in the model shop, she wanted to re-design everything in three dimensions, but she didn't have a clue what three dimensions meant! But everyone there knew how to take her work and make it three dimensional and still retain her touch. It all turned out okay, and she was grateful for that.

We would build these little models, and then we contracted Grosh Studios to build them full scale. As each section of the ride was completed, like the French or the Mexican sections, they were shipped off to Grosh Studios. They would build the sets with just shop drawings. There were no final renderings done. We only had shop drawings, which were the original sketches, and then the models themselves.

While I was working on the toys, Blaine Gibson sculpted up what we called the rubber heads. They were the actual dolls in the ride that sang and danced. They all had the same head, just painted different. Alice Davis, wife of Imagineer Marc Davis, did some marvelous work and a tremendous amount of research on the costumes to make sure they were all authentic.

Once we finished completing the sets, we took them over to a sound stage. We set it up exactly the

Inside the attraction at the World's Fair.

way it was going to be in New York. We lit it how we wanted it and added the music. We put Walt in a boat, one that had wheels, and pushed him through the entire thing so he could see how the guests would view it when it was set up in New York.

It was about this point that both Mary and I realized something was missing. The painted sets, even though they were gorgeous pieces, looked kind of flat. Especially when you compared them to all those toys and moving figures that were decorated with glitter and jewels. So we bought about $250 worth of glitter. Nowadays, $250 worth of glitter doesn't sound like a lot, but back then, it was an obscene amount. We put glue on the sets, and blew glitter all over them to give them a feeling of depth. We caught a lot of grief from the Accounting Department for spending that much on glitter (definite proof that some things never change), but it was for the best. It was a simple little trick, but it worked out really well. Another one of those happy accidents, really.

On the last few days of installation, we were all working pretty hard, but that didn't mean there wasn't time for practical jokes. One night, the workmen put a whole bunch of koi fish in the boat trough. It took us a while to get them all out of there. Another time, someone filled the trough with SuperSuds. The soapy foam went throughout the entire ride, and raised about 4 feet above the trough. It was a kick! Thankfully, it didn't damage anything.

When you stop and think, it was quite a laborious process. We had to set it up, get it all up and running for Walt to see, take it down, ship it to New York, and then set it up all over again. It was absolutely marvelous. What was really interesting, to me at least, was that we designed it, built it, and then installed it in only 9 months. No other attractions ever built by Disney have ever been done in that timeframe before…or after, for that matter!

For me, the whole thing was incredible. It was the first time I had ever been to New York and, my God, did I fall in love with that city. Mary kind of took me under her wing, and took me all around New York. She showed me everything, including the Museum of Modern Art. I spent a couple of days out in Great Neck with her family, and got to know her boys and husband really well. That was very special to me.

New York was a trip, too. It was a wild place, and we all came back with some crazy stories. I was picked up by a couple of NYC police officers once while doing my laundry in the city. The place was closed, so I was standing around, waiting for it to open when they grabbed me. Apparently, some guy was extorting the place, and they thought it was me. I pulled out my ID to show them and said, "I'm just Rolly Crump from California, in town working for Disney, and I just want to get my goddamn laundry!" They laughed at that and said, "Okay Mickey Mouse, we believe you. Now get out of here!"

And, I remember being there on opening day and my big, ugly tower was there, which was kind of a kick. It was a very proud moment for me.

There's kind of a funny story about all this, too, that most people have never heard before. Probably about a year and half prior to all of this, I was talking to my Mom and told her, "They're not keeping me busy there," meaning at Disney. I had a lot of energy back then, and I felt like I wasn't doing enough. I said to her,

TOWER, OF THE FOUR WINDS

It's A Small World, with the Tower of the Four Winds in front, on the opening day of the World's Fair.

"They're just not giving me enough to do, so I'm going to open up this little art gallery and I want you to help me run it." She agreed to do just that. This was the same little art gallery I talked about earlier. Nothing too fancy; just a little shop to show off and sell some of my work from, and make some money on the side.

One day, I said to my Mom, "I really don't know what's going to happen to me in the future, or where I'm going to end up."

"Why don't you go see Diane?" she said. Now, Diane was a psychic that my Mom had gone to for years. So, I thought, 'What the hell, let's give it a shot.' I went to Diane, and I didn't say anything. I just went without giving her any information at all. She'd read you, and check your cards, and your palm, all that stuff.

"You know, Rolly," she said to me, "in about a year and half…I think maybe in September, you're going to have 30 people working for you. You're going to be designing like you've never designed before. It's going be incredible." I was a little surprised, to be honest with you.

"You'll be flying like a big eagle," she goes on. "I see all this color in the ceiling!" I thought, 'What in God's name is this woman talking about?' I thought she was nuts. But I thanked her anyway, and went about my business.

Sure enough, the following September I'm in the middle of working on Small World, and for some entirely unknown reason, I started thinking about it. I started looking around me right then, and realized she was right. I was designing like a machine. I had 30 people working for me. I just finished the Tower of the Four Winds. And all those wonderful toys we made? Well, once we finished making them, we didn't know what to do with them. There were so many! So, we put them in clear plastic bags, and hung them from the ceiling. It was amazing!

Like I said, my Mom had been going to her for years, and I never thought anything of it until that day. I never forgot that, because I'd thought maybe my little gallery was going to get me an outside job and then

IT'S KIND OF A CUTE STORY

all of a sudden I'd be designing something for somebody else. It never dawned on me that it was going to be within Disney!

I'm really proud about the impact It's A Small World had at the New York World's Fair. I mean, I was proud of all of the shows we did for the Fair. Four of the five most popular shows were ours, so we had a lot of success. But Small World was really special to me. It was in the top three shows, despite it being the only show that charged admission, which was a measly $1 back then. This proved that the funny little idea that Walt had was a really great one. The Old Man really knew what he was doing.

Yet, none of us knew we were going to bring this back to Disneyland. We didn't realize the true significance of all these shows until Walt called us in one day and said "We own them, so we're going to bring them back and we're going put them in Disneyland."

That was a big surprise for us! But the even bigger surprise was that all the other folks who worked on Small World, like Marc and Alice Davis and so on, had all moved on to other projects. So guess who inherited bringing Small World back to Disneyland?

That's right…little old me.

Opening day of It's A Small World at the World's Fair.

Me sitting in front of It's A Small World.

CHAPTER 10

IT'S A SMALL WORLD
AT DISNEYLAND

After the World's Fair, they started disassembling the shows to ship them back to Disneyland. Everything was being packed up, and was ready to go before I knew it. The only thing was that the Tower of the Four Winds was still there. I didn't know they were going to bring the Tower back. It was my understanding that, when the World's Fair was over, they were only bringing the ride itself back. It was only later on, when they called me and told me that they didn't want to bring it back that I found out. I said, "Well, I didn't know we were bringing it back to begin with!"

You have to understand that sometimes Management wouldn't pass information like this on. I eventually got into a meeting with all these Vice Presidents. They all told me why they didn't want to bring the Tower back. And I said, "Well, yeah. I agree with you. You don't have to convince me!"

They said, "Great! We want you to tell Walt, though." They were all scared to death of telling Walt that they didn't want to bring it back. So, they put me up to the task.

Walt came into the meeting, and we carried on for about an hour. Just before he ended it, he turned to us and said, "Is there anything else?"

I said, "Yes, Walt, I wanted to talk about the Tower."

He gave me his little frown and said, "What about the Tower?"

"I don't want to bring it back," I said.

He was already aware that I didn't want to bring it back. He knew I didn't like it from the get-go, but he had a feeling that something else was up. He looked at me, and then looked at the Vice Presidents sitting around the table. His gaze landed on Joe Fowler.

"Joe, are you concerned about a propeller maybe falling off and hitting someone in the Park?" Walt asked.

"Well, yes, I am, but not really, Walt…" Joe said, and kind of fumbled through an explanation.

Walt turned to Roger Broggie next and asked, "Are you concerned about the cost to maintain the Tower?"

"Well, you know…" Roger mumbled, and sort of trailed off.

Walt knew that every one of those guys sitting there had set me up to tell him. They all had their own concerns about it, but he knew just by the way they were sitting there that they didn't want to tell him themselves.

Eventually, he said, "Okay, we won't bring it back."

All the Vice Presidents were out of there in two seconds flat, before he had a chance to change his mind. It was just Walt and I left in the room.

"Does it really bother you that we're not bringing it back?" I asked him.

"No, not at all," he said with a smile. He knew where the Vice Presidents were coming from, but he just wanted to tease them a little bit and make them sweat, and that was fine by me!

The Tower was cut into 2 foot sections and thrown into the ocean. That's been the rumor circulating around for years, but it's the truth. It probably wouldn't be thought to be environmentally sound to do something like that today, but back then we didn't really understand the ramifications of it. So, somewhere out in the Atlantic, a bunch of fish now call the Tower of the Four Winds their home.

I do know that Bob Gurr does have a piece from the original Tower, though. Down toward the bottom, there was a little carousel of animals that went round and round. When they were taking it apart, Bob said he wanted one of those animals and shipped it back home. So, part of it still lives on today.

Like I mentioned earlier, though, most of the principal players who brought Small World to life at the World's Fair had moved on to other projects. I was the only one still available, so I was put in charge of getting it into place at Disneyland. I sort of inherited the project, which I thought was just wonderful.

Even though I was in charge of installing the attraction, Mary Blair was still the stylist. We were putting it on a very large piece of land, and I needed something much more fanciful for the façade than what we had at the World's Fair. So, I contacted Mary and asked her to draw me some sketches of what she thought the façade should look like. She sent about six sketches over, which were all wonderful.

Mary took the first crack at designing the façade model. She decided she wanted it to be like a little girl playing with blocks. It was interesting, and she spent about six weeks working on it with a bunch of other gals. The problem was, while her style was amazing, she still didn't understand designing in three dimensions.

We had a meeting with Walt one day on what the façade would look like, and Mary gave her little presentation, showing off her model. As you know, Walt, if he saw something he didn't like, he wouldn't come out and say "I don't like that." Instead, he would say, "You know what? Maybe let's try it from a different angle." And that's exactly what happened here. He kept looking at the model, kind of frowning, and you could just see in his face that he wasn't buying off on it.

After that, we went back to the main model, because Mary was also asked to design the Islands section for the ride. The Islands weren't represented in the World's Fair version, so we were trying to make it fit in with the rest of the ride. It was only natural that Mary try that one, too. She decided to put carpet all over the sets, and it just didn't work at all with her style. Walt looked at those, too, and said, "You know, Mary, we're going to have to really take a hard look at this to figure it out."

Well, poor little Mary went over to Alphonse, a local bar, had six martinis, and caught an airplane home!

I went to Dick Irvine, who was the Supervising Art Director at the time, and told him, "I know what

Early model for the façade of It's A Small World.

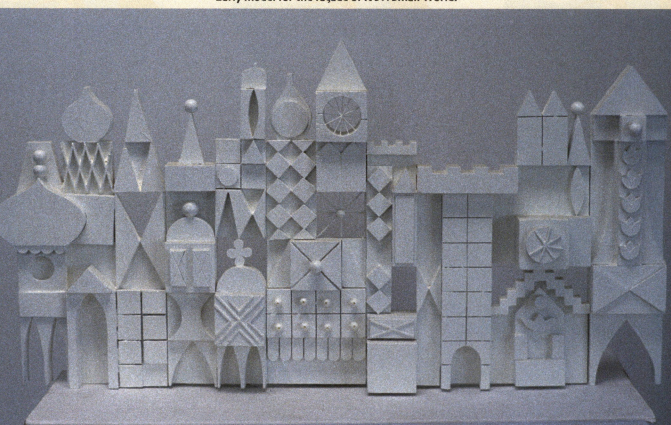

Walt wants with the façade. I'll do it for you, but I don't want to answer to anybody but Walt." In those days, a lot of the architects at WED were voicing their opinions, and it got to be a little bit of a mish-mosh. I knew that if I started something, and other people could put their little fingers on it, it would wind up being a mess. But Dick agreed, and I went ahead.

Actually, while Mary was doing her models, I was doing my own on the side. I would take her drawings, which were geometrical in a lot of ways, and just trace them. I built these little block models directly from her drawings. I only did them so I could show Mary how she should be approaching it, to help her out. When I gave them to her, she looked at them and said, "Oh, that's just great, Rolly!" And then she just plopped them down, right in the middle of all the little blocks she'd built, and that just made it even worse!

I enlisted the assistance of Fred Joerger to help build the model. We built this amazing half-inch scale model out of cardboard in seven days, which was record time. Not to take anything away from Mary, but that's because we knew what we were doing. During that whole 2 year period working with Mary on Small World for the World's Fair, I'd just been studying everything she'd been doing. Her style just kind of flowed out of me, and that really helped when building the model. It was probably one of the easiest things I've ever done in my life.

I remember when we put the Leaning Tower of Pisa on there. Obviously, everything else on the model was vertical. People would always look at it and say, "Hey, that one's crooked!" and I'd say, "Of course it is! It's the Leaning Tower of Pisa!"

This is where another cute little story comes in. Fred and I were getting ready to show the model to Walt. We had it on this very small table, and we were trying to position where all the landscaping was going to go. There wasn't any space left on the table, so we set the miniature trees on top of the building, and just picked them off as we worked out places for them. We were in the middle of trying to figure it out when Walt walked in, early for the meeting. He looked at what he saw, and approved.

"You know what I really like? That idea of trees on the roof, that's incredible. Nobody will know there's a building there!" he said to us. And we just quickly replied, "Oh, yes, we thought it was a pretty good idea, too!" We couldn't help but burst out laughing, though. We confessed why they were really there, but Walt still thought it was a good idea.

"I don't care. I love it. Let's do it." When they opened up Small World Disneyland, we did have trees all over the roof. That was another one of those happy accidents. But, in time, they became a nightmare for Maintenance to deal with, so they disappeared.

Like I mentioned earlier, we didn't bring the Tower of the Four Winds back to Disneyland with us. The one thing that I've always loved about Disneyland is that there is always something moving. Whether it's one of the streetcars going down Main Street, AstroJets in Tomorrowland, or the old Skyway, there was always this feeling of motion that I just adored. We managed to achieve that at the World's Fair with the Tower of the Four Winds. At Disneyland, though…that was another story. When I looked at the façade for Small World, I thought, "It's 60 feet high and 300 feet long. Nothing is moving, and it's just as dull as can be."

Thinking back to my earlier projects, I decided to put propellers on there. That really gave it some life. In fact, when I showed Walt the finished model, I had a fan running so the propellers would give that sense of kinetic energy. I wanted Walt to experience what I was going for. He loved it.

The original model had a bare platform out in front. Walt looked at it and said, "What are you going to put on the platform, Rolly?"

I instantly went to my go-to answer: "I don't know."

But something had to go there.

We went back and forth on possible suggestions for a few minutes, one of which was a band. That was met with, "We can't afford a band there every day! Besides, it'll just be empty when they aren't playing!"

Eventually Walt said, "What about a clock?"

I immediately called Mary Blair again.

"Mary, draw me a picture of a clock!"

She drew a small black-and-white sketch, that looked similar to the Tower of the Four Winds, on a napkin from an airplane. I still have that original sketch, framed, in my office at home.

From that basic sketch, I built an elaborate model with music, a working clock and little figures coming out the back. When it came time for Walt to come down to look at the finished model, Dick Irvine came by and said he wanted to see the clock first.

So I showed him the model, and ran the whole show for him. He looked at it and said that he didn't think it was the right clock for the façade.

"Maybe I'll have Marc Davis re-design it," he said.

"Are you out of your mind?" I asked him.

"Well, it doesn't have a little rooster coming out to crow and it doesn't have any bells ringing. It's not a clock!" He was thinking of what a typical European clock looked like, which clearly mine was not. I was getting a little angry, but I had a thought.

"At least let Walt see it first," I asked him. He agreed.

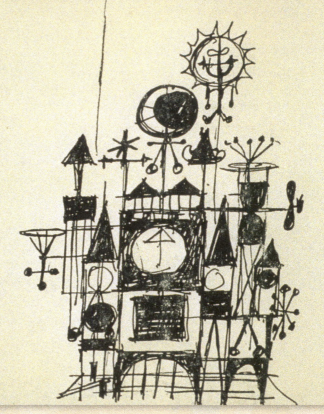

The original drawing of the clock that Mary Blair drew on a napkin while on a flight home. It's currently framed, in my Disney Room.

A little while later, he came by with Walt to show it off. I ran the whole show, and Walt just looked at it. Dick got a smile on his face, thinking that Walt was going to agree with him.

"Run it again, Rolly," Walt said. So I ran it again for him. When it finished, Dick went to Walt and

Explaining to Walt the new scene for It's A Small World.

IT'S KIND OF A CUTE STORY

told him he was going to get Marc Davis to re-design it. He started rattling off all the reasons why, but Walt stopped him straight away.

"I like it exactly the way it is," he told him. With that, Dick shut up.

It was a pretty sophisticated model, which was good because Walt really liked seeing how the final product would work. He was pleased with it, and so was I. He took another look at it again, and had an idea.

"How many figures do you have coming out that clock?"

I only had 9 at that time, but that wasn't enough for Walt.

"Don't you realize there are 24 hours in a day?" Well, of course, that made more sense.

"I don't want them coming out the side, either. I want them coming out the front, so people can see them."

So I added more figures to make it an even 24, and I raised the clock so they could come out the front. And you know what? It looked just marvelous like that.

I went to Jimmy MacDonald, who did all these great sound effects over at the Disney Studios. I took the clock model with me to show him all the different pieces that I wanted to have sound effects. Stuff like the doors opening, and the little trumpeters coming out, and the numbers going in and out to let you know what time it was. He used to crack me up with this one sound effect. I don't even remember where it went at this point, but he took a little BB bullet, and put it inside a balloon. He started shaking it, and the BB would roll around in the balloon and make this crazy noise. I just loved it. It was amazing how he would come up with those effects.

The morning that Walt was going to come over to check out the façade model and give it the final buy off, all the other designers decided they didn't want to be there. Dick Irvine made sure I was ready for Walt but then left with the rest of them. For some reason, they decided that they didn't want to be there, in case he didn't like it, so they left me to fend for myself. But that was fine. I was ready for him.

Walt came over, and leaned on the big platform that we had the façade on for him to look at. He looked at it for three or four minutes and didn't say a word. Just staring, studying, going over every detail in his head.

He turned to me and said, "Rolly, do you have any regrets or anything about this that bothers you? What do you think about it?"

I said, "I think it's fine. I think it's just the way it should be."

"So you have no regrets?" he asked.

I said, "No, Sir."

"Well, build the goddamn thing then!" he said, and walked away. That was Walt's own way of saying, "Good work."

Unfortunately, all those wonderful models got destroyed. Well, everything except for that first clock we did. They never kept anything at WED, so they just started throwing everything away. But I wasn't going to let them throw that one away. It was small enough for me to take home, and that's just what I did. I still have it today!

When it came time to install the façade, I went to the Maintenance department to ask for some advice.

"What are the things that you want me to be careful of?" I asked.

The first thing they said was, "Don't paint it in color, because it'll just fade away. We'd have to go up there to repaint it every year, and that's just not in our maintenance budget."

Now, with the model I built, everything was in full color. But, heeding their advice, I agreed to just paint it white. That's when I decided to accent it with gold leaf. White was a fine color, but I wanted a little bit of life to it. Gold leaf never tarnishes, so it would last forever provided nobody put their oily fingers on it. I thought that would help Maintenance out a lot.

During the installation, we used so much of it that we used up all the gold leaf available in the U.S.! We had to get some from Germany to finish the job. Unfortunately, for some reason or another, the German gold leaf tarnished after a few months of being up there. Luckily, the U.S. had replenished its supply by then, and we were able to replace it.

It was my idea to put those doilies on the façade, too. Along with the propellers, I glued a whole bunch

The original scale model for the It's A Small World façade, featuring a working clock.

of gold doilies all over the façade model to give it more of a spark of life. When you're looking at Small World, to the left, there's a big doily in a circle. There's an interesting story behind that one.

When we were installing the façade, a security guard came up to me and asked if I was the guy who did the design. I said I was, and he said, "Well, one of those doilies is upside-down." I said, "What?!" He'd just happened to notice it looked off when he was walking by, and wanted to mention it to me.

I went over to look, and sure enough, it was upside-down. So we went over to the contractor who had all the drawings and plans out. But he insisted it was right. After looking at his plans, I realized he was looking at it the wrong way! I turned the sheet around, and he looked at it and said, "My God, you're right. It is upside-down!"

"Well, can you fix it?" I asked him.

"We'd have to cut that entire doily out, and then reattach it. It would take a few days. Nobody will probably even notice it if we leave it."

I thought to myself, 'Well, maybe he's right. Maybe I won't have to worry about it.'

The security guy was standing there with us while we were talking about it, but he got up to go look at it himself. He came back, and he said, "You know, there are only four bolts holding it in there. Everything is symmetrical, so if you just loosen those bolts, take it out, and turn it right side up, you'll be fine."

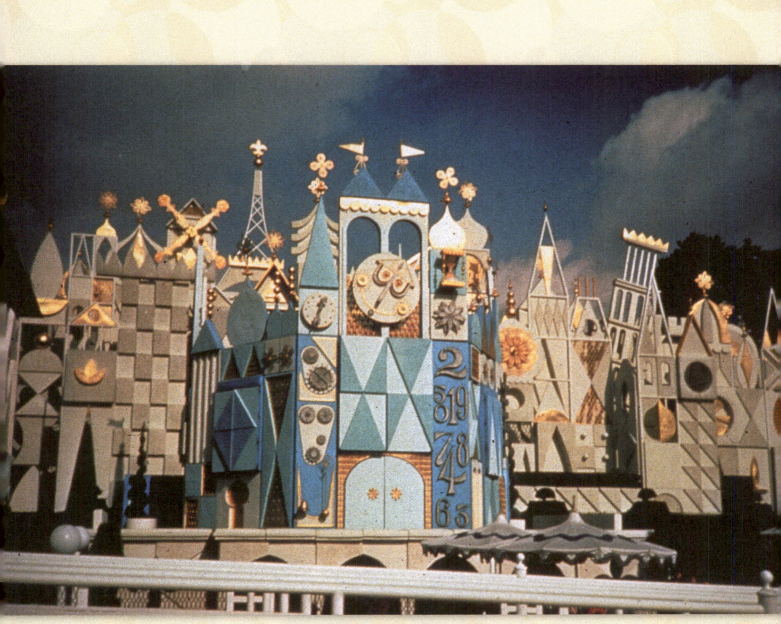

It's A Small World, as seen in the early 1970s.

We went back to the contractor to ask him if he'd do it, and he said he would. He got a cherry picker, went up there, and did it in less than 5 minutes. I can't thank that security guy enough for saving the façade!

You always hear about Walt being a pretty level-headed guy. He rarely lost his temper, but when he did, boy, did you know it! The one time that really sticks out in my mind was when he unloaded on Dick Irvine which, of course, I thought was just wonderful. Where Small World is now at Disneyland, there used to be a train station. In order for Small World to move into that area, we would have to do something about it. Someone suggested moving the tracks a little bit, and having the train pass in front of the façade of the attraction. Walt liked that idea, and decided that's what we were going to do.

For some reason, Dick didn't like that decision, and he made it pretty clear that he wasn't happy about it. Walt, Dick, and I were walking to the WED building one day, and Dick brought it up.

"You know Walt, I really think we shouldn't move the tracks."

"I like the idea. We're moving them," Walt replied.

"Yes, but I really think they should stay where they are," Dick came back at him.

"The decision has been made, Dick, we're moving them."

"I just don't think it's a good idea," Dick just kept saying.

Walt turned to him and just came undone. He was really angry! He didn't like the idea that once a decision was made and agreed upon, somebody else would come back and take a whack at it. Needless to say, by the time we got over to WED, everything was alright between Walt and Dick again. But Walt had to let him know who was in charge, and that his decision was final.

As far as I was concerned, the only people that got yelled at by Walt deserved it. They went for that third strike, and you just don't do that with the boss. But I thought to myself, "If he ever talks to me like that, I'll have to leave to go home and never come back!"

Another funny story is about when we were working on the exit of the ride. I was designing a portico-like building for Bank of America. They were all over the world at the time, and they were sponsoring the ride, so they wanted a little building where they could explain their international policy and so on to guests. I was working with Bill Justice on the model for the building, and we were brainstorming ideas. I said to him, "You know, this represents a bank. Why don't you put Indian head coins all around the base?" It was just this random idea I had, but he went ahead and did it. I thought it looked pretty nice, but when Walt came over to see, he didn't approve.

"What the hell are these Indian head coins doing on there?" he said, while looking right at Bill. I didn't want to get him in trouble, so I said, "Excuse me, Sir, that was my idea. I told Bill to do that." But that didn't stop Walt from chewing him out.

"What the hell else are you doing, Bill?" Walt just kind of wanted to get a rise out of him, though. He didn't like the design, but he was always pushing people to make things better. Walt knew that I wouldn't let anybody else take the blame for something that I did, so he was impressed by that.

Another great little story about that Bank of America building is about when we made the model of it out of cardboard. Walt and John Wise came over to check it out and said, "You know, that doesn't look very sturdy to me."

Walt turned to him and said, "Don't worry, John. We're not going to make the real thing out of cardboard."

After we opened the ride, people loved it. But, it still generated a lot of scrutiny from the public. You wouldn't believe the questions and letters that we received about it.

For example, there was one letter from Australia that stated, "The koala bears that you have in the Island section would die climbing those palm trees because they live off eucalyptus leaves. We would like to see eucalyptus leaves in the koala's paws."

Well, my first reaction was, "Where did you ever see a koala bear that was made out of yellow chicken feathers?" But, believe it or not, real eucalyptus leaves were put in the koalas' paws in case that guest ever came back.

Me sitting in front of It's A Small World.

We also got a letter from someone claiming there was nothing representing the Jewish heritage in the ride. Ironically, my boss at the time, Marty Sklar, was Jewish, so he wanted to appease that guest, too.

I got to work, researching what would be appropriate for the ride. What I mean by 'appropriate' is that all the dolls were costumed to conform to a specific timeframe. We had to have this new doll fit in with the rest. We costumed one of the boys with a Jewish flute, made a little set for him, and put him in the attraction. We certainly could've put a rabbi in there, and that would've read a lot easier

IT'S KIND OF A CUTE STORY

Me standing in front of It's A Small World shortly before it opened at Disneyland.

for people, but that would've looked out of place with the rest of the attraction.

Funny enough, not too much later after that, we got another letter from the same person asking, "Where's the little Jewish boy?" We took a picture of the doll, photocopied my research, and mailed the entire package back to the concerned guest.

It's funny, because the same thing occurred during the design process of It's A Small World for Tokyo Disneyland. We were instructed to make the Oriental section Japanese only, nothing else. This sweet Japanese girl I was working with volunteered to take the project on herself. She claimed she knew exactly what they wanted, so we went for it. We built a scale model to represent traditional Japanese culture in just a few weeks, and then sent it to Tokyo. The feedback we received wasn't quite what we expected: "What the hell is this? This isn't Japanese!" It's unbelievable sometimes!

A lot of people ask me about the changes made to the ride recently, by adding the Disney characters to it. Honestly, I'm not all that bothered by it. I know there was a big fuss over it, but when I saw it, I thought they did a beautiful job. They really worked to make sure they blended into the show seamlessly. You wouldn't even know they were there if you weren't looking for them.

As for the ride, it was great to get it into a place where it can now live forever. I'm glad people can still enjoy it, all these years later. I'm really happy with the fact that I was able to sneak the Mary Blair doll that I had done for the World's Fair into the Disneyland version. It's still there, on the Eiffel Tower, after all these years. I also hid something new in there, too, as a kind of tribute to someone I was very close with at the time. People always told us we were like two peas in a pod, so I made us exactly that! In the first scene, off to the right, are two peas in a pod, hanging out. It's amazing to me that these little personal touches of mine have stayed there all these years.

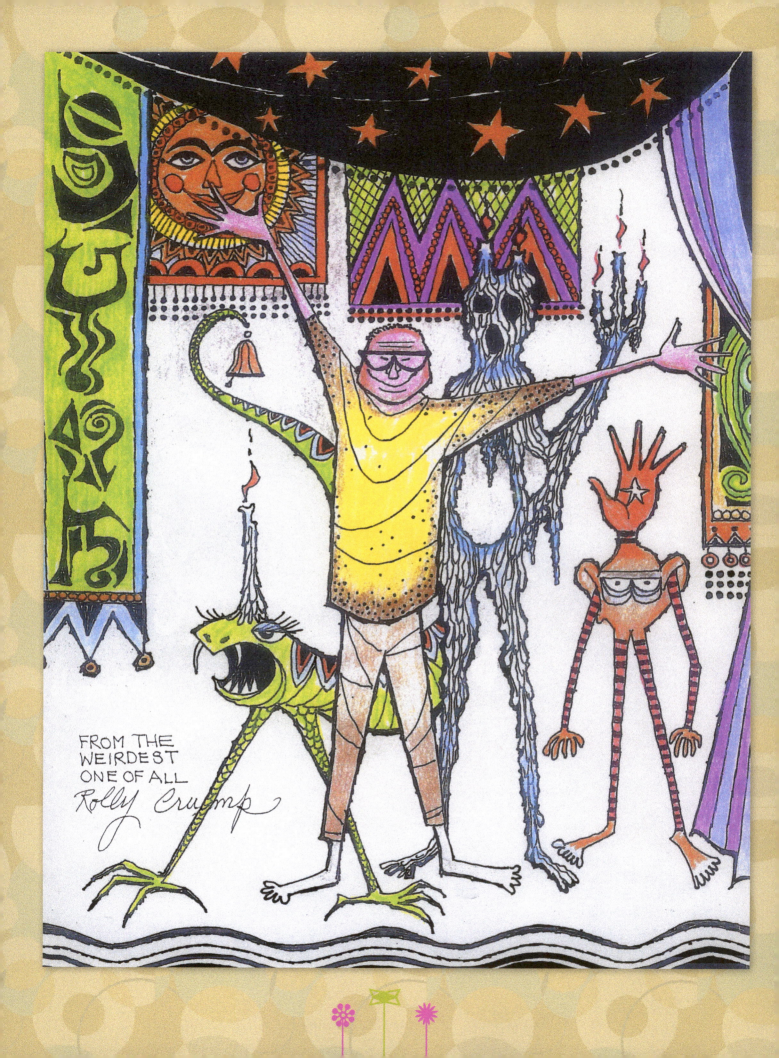

FROM THE
WEIRDEST
ONE OF ALL
Rolly Crump

CHAPTER 11

Museum Of the Weird

fter we came back from the World's Fair, and It's A Small World was in place at Disneyland, people went back to work on the things they were doing before. So, that meant I was back to working on the Haunted Mansion. At this point, I realized that everybody that I've been working with was thinking of it like a typical haunted house. You know, of *The Cat and the Canary* kind, with shutters that banged, footprints on the ceiling, secret panels, and all the things I thought were pretty corny. I didn't want the Mansion to be based on these heavily used clichés, but it was going to be unless I did something about it.

I started doing sketches based on some films I was inspired by at the time. I imagined using the human body as part of the architecture of the place, much like in Jean Cocteau's 1946 film *Beauty and the Beast*. I was also pretty heavily influenced by *Juliet of the Spirits* by Federico Fellini. I wanted arms coming out of the wall to hold torches, faces over the fireplace that blew smoke at you as you walked by…very surreal stuff.

I started to come up with all these really crazy concepts, and I thought it would be interesting to put them all on display somewhere in the Mansion. One of them was a candle man. I drew it so his fingers were the candles, with wax dripping down. He would appear to be melting right in front of you!

The Mistress of Evil was another character I came up with, and I was going to have her appear in an archway, up on a balcony. There were going to be flames all around her, but made out of China Silk. When you had wind blowing through China Silk, and lit it just right, it looked like the real thing. She would be lifted up in the air, and she'd open her arms real wide and start screaming like Maleficent did. Just really creepy and weird stuff I had her doing.

There was also an exhibit in there that I was going to call the Seven Sins of Man. It was a Devil standing there, with 7 mirrors in front of him. He'd be reflected back in all of them, looking normal. Then the lights would dim, and in one of the mirrors, he would be reflected back with a Pepper's Ghost image to represent one of the sins. This would go on for all 7 mirrors, before eventually going back to normal. It would have been a neat, but complicated, trick.

I also started designing all kinds of altars to place around the Mansion. You know, the kind of place where someone would go if they wanted to put a hex on somebody. They'd have to offer something to an altar to get their wish granted. I came up with a bunch of those.

Opposite: From The Weirdest One Of All—Self-portrait, with some of my weirdest creations.

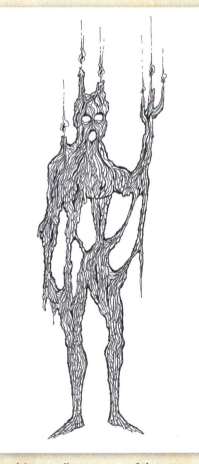

The melting candle man, one of the most famous images from the Museum (redrawn from the original sketch).

The Mistress of Evil, just before her screams would let loose (redrawn from the original sketch).

A mirror from the Museum of the Weird (redrawn from the original sketch).

The chair that would have struck up a conversation with you (redrawn from the original sketch).

One of the things I wanted to be in the Mansion was a library. In fact, I wanted it to be the very first room you walked into. All these things in there were going to talk to each other from across the room, and you'd literally be in the middle of their conversation. I would use projections and Pepper's Ghost to get moving faces on everything, either from behind or in front of them, depending on where you were standing. The whole room would just come to life before your eyes.

Another room I planned was a séance room, like the Haunted Mansion has now. But mine had a chair

One of the rooms intended for the Museum of the Weird (redrawn from the original sketch).

IT'S KIND OF A CUTE STORY

Man-eating plant design that eventually became the basis for the Haunted Mansion's wallpaper (redrawn from the original sketch).

in there, which stood up to talk to you while you were in there. There were also man-eating plants in there. Claude Coats took the man-eating plant design, and used it as the basis for that famous wallpaper in the Haunted Mansion.

There was also a gypsy wagon that, much like the Small World clock, would come to life every so often, and put on a sort of show. Flames would shoot out, doors would fly open, bells would ring and all sorts of magical, weird little stuff would happen. I also wanted it to use "black art" to have things float in the air, and move in and out of the cart, to kind of throw people off more. Black art is something you see in the theater a lot, where there are props on the stage, but the curtain is black and the lights are dim. Somebody dressed all in black could come on stage, and start moving items around. You'd swear the stuff was actually moving by itself because you couldn't see the person in black! It's a simple little illusion and I thought it would give the gypsy cart an extra weird quality.

Throughout the entire Mansion, I wanted all sorts of weird architecture and themes. A few of the rooms would have chandeliers hanging down, and columns off to the side. I didn't want it to draw your attention right away, but if you took the time to look at it, you'd see all the little details that were added in. Again, I was influenced by *Beauty and the Beast*, and I was going to have human body parts make up the architecture. There was a woman's face hidden in the chandelier, and you'd only see it if you put it all together in your mind. The columns were all made up by weird looking body parts; arms and legs literally holding the building together.

Thinking about the atmosphere in general, though, I didn't want things to be obvious. I wanted to

The gypsy cart that would amaze guests with its floating trinkets (redrawn from the original sketch).

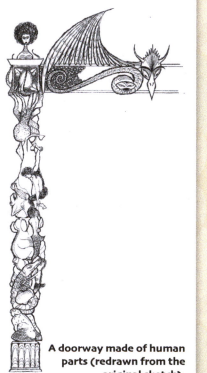

A doorway made of human parts (redrawn from the original sketch).

A beast man, one of the many denizens intended for the Museum of the Weird (redrawn from the original sketch).

A reptilian creature intended for the Museum of the Weird (redrawn from the original sketch).

intertwine the weird stuff, so that you had to look twice to see it. Sort of a "Wait, is that what I think it is?" moment when you look at a chair, and then realize it's made of bones.

So, it was subtle. Nothing jumping out at you, like they were doing for the rest of the Mansion. Another good example of that was the guy I made out of all different animal parts. He was just a statue standing there when you would first walk into a room. A silhouette, even. But then as you got close to him, you'd look and realize, "Oh my God, his leg is a fish!"

I really wanted to give people a sense of discovery in there, like they were finding all of this stuff out on their own. Nobody was going to point it out to you, so the more you explored, the more you'd see. I think something like that would keep people coming back, trying to explore all the nooks and crannies to find all the weird stuff they could.

As I was planning this whole thing out and doing the sketches, Jack Ferges, who was one of the model builders, came over to check them out. Now, you have to understand that Jack was this huge guy. Each of his fingers was about the size of a banana! But he was one of the most talented model builders I have ever met. He used to make these tiny models that were impossibly intricate. No one could figure out how he could do that with such huge hands. I remember Walt was watching him work once, and he said, "I'd love to know your secret!"

I said, "Walt, you mean you don't know how he does it?"

Walt turned to me and said, "No. How?"

And I told him, "Well, Jack just unscrews his giant hands, because hidden inside are these little tiny hands that allow him to work with all these small models."

Walt just kind of looked at me, and gave me his signature "Oh, Roland…" catchphrase, which he did when he knew my jokes were a little off-the-wall. I still find that moment pretty funny.

Jack came over to check out my drawings. He told me he didn't have anything to do, and wanted to know if he could build some models based on my sketches. I agreed, because I wanted to see how they would translate three dimensionally, and he just did a marvelous job. There's that one photo of me, which you may have seen, with one of the models in my hand, pretending to work on it. They did that for the *World of Color* television show but, the truth was, Jack was behind all those wonderful models. Unfortunately, most of them were destroyed over time. Some may still exist in the Disney Archives somewhere, but a lot of them are long gone.

IT'S KIND OF A CUTE STORY

One of the rooms intended for the Museum of the Weird (redrawn from the original sketch).

At the time, the rest of WED was assigned to work on the Haunted Mansion. It was kind of divided into two camps: the rest of WED developing the look of the attraction, and then me with my little 'Museum of the Weird,' as it ended up being called around the workshop.

When we had a meeting with Walt to go over our progress so far, we laid everything out for him to see. Dick Irvine put me and all my weird things over in the corner, behind where Walt was going to sit, so he wouldn't see it. Walt walked into the room, with all this stuff for the Haunted Mansion in front of him, and took a seat. It was about a 3 hour meeting to go over everything with Walt. At the end, Dick said, "Well, I guess that's it," and started to escort Walt out.

But Walt noticed my things in the corner and said, "What's that over there?"

"Well, that's what Rolly's working on," Dick said.

"Well, what's that Rolly's working on?" Walt asked.

"We don't know. You ask him," Dick replied, kind of embarrassed.

So Walt walked over and said, "Okay, what are you working on Rolly?" I just kind of looked at him and said, "Honestly, I don't know!"

We pushed our chairs right up to where my things were, and he started looking all of it over.

"This stuff is really weird, Rolly," he said to me. I told him I knew it was, but I felt that the Haunted Mansion really needed something other than just the straight ghost stuff everyone else was working on. I started to tell him all about *Beauty and the Beast*, and how I thought the Mansion would be a better experience if it had similar things like that in it.

Walt just looked kind of blank for a few moments and then said, "Yeah, Rolly, but how are we going to use this stuff?" I told him I really had no clue. This exchange went on for about five minutes, and then Walt

Aquarium with ghost fish (redrawn from the original sketch).

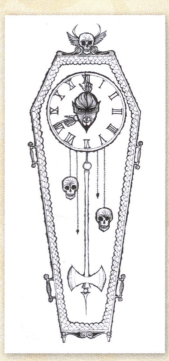

Grandfather Coffin Clock (redrawn from the original sketch).

finally said, "That's it. I'm out of here!" He just stood up, and left!

Everybody came up to me after that, saying, "We told you this stuff was too weird. We knew Walt wouldn't like it." I didn't care, though. I was having fun. I was just trying to throw a little more imagination into the Mansion.

I came into work the next morning at 7 AM to get an early start on my day. When I got to my chair, I found Walt sitting there, still dressed in the same clothes from the day before. He looked at me, and the first words out of his mouth were, "You son of a bitch."

I said, "Whoa, what?" I was trying to figure out what I did wrong.

"I didn't get an ounce of sleep last night because of all those sketches you showed me," he started to explain to me.

"Oh God, I'm sorry," I said. I didn't mean to mess up his night with all my weird ideas.

But he looked at me with that smile again and said, "No, no, don't be sorry. I've got this idea for it!"

So Walt sat there and explained to me that he wanted to put this little Museum of the Weird at the end of the Mansion, so people would have to walk through it before getting to the exit. He wanted the backstory to be that someone collected all this weird stuff from around the world, and we shipped it to Disneyland, and that's how the Museum wound up being inside the Haunted Mansion.

I said, "God, Walt, that's great!" Jack Ferges joined us at that point, once he noticed we were huddled over the models, and the three of us started laying out these plans. I did confide to Walt at one point, though, thinking that I went a little TOO far with all this. I let my imagination run away from me. Walt was such a sweetheart about it, and said to me, "No Rolly, you go as far out as you want. I'm the one who will bring you back."

A little while later, Dick Irvine showed up. He's got two cups of coffee in his hands; one for him and one for Walt. He was a little bit nervous because he thought Walt got there before he did. When Dick pulled in and saw Walt's car in the parking lot, he thought, 'Oh God,' and ran inside. So here he was, trying to find Walt to give him his coffee. Walt motioned him over and told him to gather up the rest of the guys who were in the meeting the day before. When they all showed up, Walt went into a half hour presentation on the Museum of the Weird.

At the end of it, he turned to me and said, "God, I'm really looking forward to the Museum of the Weird!" Then he looked at Dick and said, "I'm going to go home and go to bed now." With that, he turned around and left.

IT'S KIND OF A CUTE STORY

Everyone just kind of stared for a few moments before turning to me and saying, "God, Rolly, we knew that you had something there!" But that whole thing just showed me how beautiful the Old Man was. He was always open to these crazy ideas, and he worked with you to make them work.

Unfortunately, Walt's death brought a halt to any further development on the Museum. Though, it did get the spotlight for a bit on the *Walt Disney's Wonderful World of Color* TV show. That helped earn its place as one of the greatest unbuilt attractions among Disney fans. If Walt hadn't passed, I'm convinced that the Museum of the Weird would have been built.

Like everything else at Imagineering, ideas never die; they just get put away for a while. Some of my weird concepts did make it into the Haunted Mansion, if only indirectly. Those wall sconces of arms holding torches are right out of my designs. And like I said, even that infamous wallpaper, with the eyes that look at you, is eerily similar to drawings of a man-eating plant I did. So, a little bit of my weirdness did creep in, over time.

In the new Haunted Mansion queue at Walt Disney World, there is a crypt that has some Museum of the Weird drawings on it. It's the one that is double-sided, with the organ you can play. Both sides have instruments that, when you touch them, play a familiar, ghostly tune. The first side you see has all normal instruments on it, but when you make your way to the other side, you'll see all these far out designs. Most of them are similar, if not exactly identical, to a lot of the things I did when designing the Museum. While it would have been nice to see the Museum as Walt and I pictured it come to life, it's still nice to see it live on in some form.

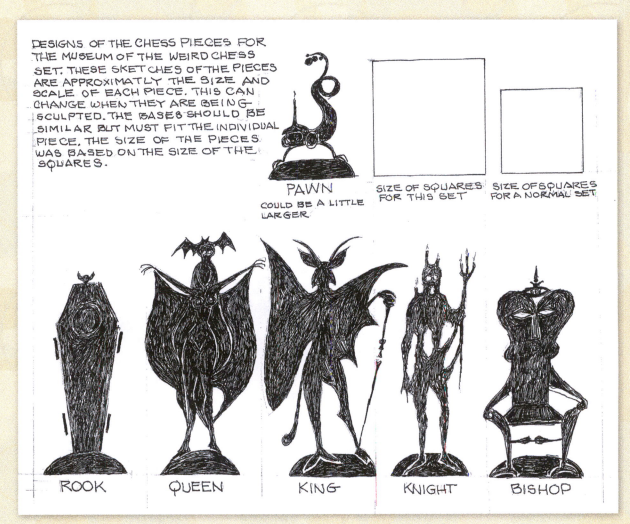

Concept for a Museum of the Weird chess set that I designed a few years ago.

CHAPTER 12

TOMORROWLAND RE-DESIGN 1967

One of the things that the Company was working on toward the end of my Museum of the Weird stint was a re-design of Tomorrowland. I was doing a little model of the Museum's gypsy wagon one day when Walt walked in and asked what I was doing. I told him, and he said, "Wait a minute, we're building a new Tomorrowland. I want you working on that!"

I couldn't fight with the boss, so I said fine, and called up Dick Irvine to get an assignment. He huffed for a bit, since we didn't really see eye to eye on anything. But, since Walt told me this is what I should be working on, Dick had to give me something.

Eventually, he assigned me a whole bunch of stuff. I wound up working on a temporary bandstand where Space Mountain was supposed to go (which ultimately became a permanent structure known as Tomorrowland Terrace, where the stage is hidden underground until show time), new ticket booths, and two shops: Mickey's Mart and Mad Hatter. I had no idea who was doing all these things before I came along, but this person was taken off the project because Walt wanted me.

I started with Mickey's Mart, because I thought that was the one that was going to take the most work. I called Jack Olsen, who was the head of Merchandise at the time, because he also helped me out when I re-did Adventureland Bazaar.

Scale model of the Tomorrowland bandstand.
Opposite: **The temporary Tomorrowland bandstand that eventually became permanent.**

I asked him what kind of merchandise they were going to be selling in Mickey's Mart, and he told me it was going to mostly be plush stuffed animals. That meant everything was going to be brightly colored. In order to contrast that, and to kind of give it a more futuristic look, I decided the entire shop should be in black and white. I had enlarged these wonderful old photos of Mickey Mouse that I had found, and hung them from the ceiling.

The ceiling in there was pretty high. Again, to give it a kind of weird, futuristic look, I hung a long electrical cord with lights from the ceiling, and brought it all the way down to the counter. These strings with bulb lighting were the only light source, and they just looked pretty neat. Maintenance and Operations were worried they were going to blow away in the wind, but they wound up never having any problems with it.

Jack Olsen was a swell guy. Every time I'd go down to Disneyland to work for a few days, rather than renting a motel, Jack was kind enough to let me stay at his house. He had a pool table in his living room, and every night we'd come home and shoot pool into the wee hours of the morning.

He came home with this fantastic motorcycle one day after work, and I just fell in love with it.

"You should get one," he said. "We'll go riding together." I told him that there was no way that I could afford one, but he came up with a pretty clever idea.

"You know those sculptures you do? Why don't you make one out of the leftover wood from Mickey's Mart, and I'll buy it from you. We can put it in the corner and use it as a hat stand," he said.

I thought it was a pretty good idea. He said to charge him whatever I thought a motorcycle might cost. I estimated it would probably be about $500 and he said that was fine.

So I made the sculpture myself out of plywood, painted it white, and sold it to him for $500! Clearly no one checked

The top of the bandstand, which is the only thing guests would see until the stage rose from beneath it.

My re-design for the Mad Hatter.

Interior views of Mickey's Mart.

IT'S KIND OF A CUTE STORY

Another temporary Tomorrowland bandstand.

accounting all that closely at the time. With that extra cash, I got a motorcycle for myself. After that, Jack and I would go out riding together all over. We even took a trip to Mexico once, which was really kind of fun.

I also wound up helping Bill Evans, who was in charge of landscaping at Disneyland, with the floral arrangement near the entrance of Tomorrowland. He used to always talk about this landscaper in Europe that did these wonderful, swirly, almost psychedelic patterns.

We went out there together, and he got up on this wooden platform so he could see the whole thing, and I stood in the dirt with a shovel. He kind of directed me along, and I made an entire pattern using just a shovel and my mind. We didn't have any drawings to work from; we just kind of did it as we went along. It took us a while, but we laid out this beautiful pattern with only one tool and a bit of imagination.

The flower guys came in a few hours later to drop everything off. Bill and I got down on our hands and knees and planted every single flower there. We both thought it was a really beautiful way to be drawn into Tomorrowland, and it was different from the usual stuff we did. Every year after that, they always brought new flowers in, but they kept the same pattern. They didn't even change it one inch. It was spectacular to see that come back every year. I was always really proud of that.

We finished the Tomorrowland re-design in spring of 1967, fairly soon after Walt had passed away. Walt had been guiding it, and we felt we had done everything that he had wanted. The night before the grand re-opening, we all went down there to do a final check. There was a ribbon stretched in front of the entry way that they were going to cut the next day to celebrate the opening. We all stood there in a daze, because it really hit us that that was the last thing that we'd ever work with Walt on. We didn't have a clue what the next thing was going to be. That was probably my saddest moment at Disney.

The flower design at the entrance to Tomorrowland that I did under the direction of Bill Evans.

My re-design of a Tomorrowland ticket booth.

Rolly hard at work on his latest project.

CHAPTER 13

Disney on Parade

In the late 1960s, Disney Management decided they wanted to try their hand at a traveling show. They didn't want to do it on ice, which was all the rage at the time, but rather in an arena. And so *Disney on Parade* was born. Bob Jani was the head of entertainment at Disneyland at the time, and he was the guy who really came up with the idea to begin with. He put together a team of us that also included that Big Mooseketeer, Roy Williams. We all packed into a tiny trailer behind Disneyland, and got to work on the show. I was in charge of all the backgrounds, props, and set design.

Since it was a traveling show, they had to drive the entire thing around the country in these big semi-trucks. It wasn't easy to move, because it was like a circus on steroids, with all the things they needed to bring. The problem was Bob went a little overboard with what he wanted. He really went nuts, because he thought this was such a grand idea and that he could do whatever he wanted. We had no idea how the hell we were going to ship everything around, because Disney had only budgeted us at half a dozen trucks for the show.

So I sat down, and decided we had to put all of our models and props on a table to measure everything out. We could use those measurements to see how many trucks we would need to transport everything. By the time I was done figuring it all out, I realized it was going to take us at least 20 trucks! We obviously were going to have to cut back.

Bob didn't like that idea one bit. In fact, even after we re-designed everything to fit into the 6 trucks we did have, he hated it. But eventually he realized he didn't have a choice, and we had to scale back. There was no way to do the show he really wanted.

Before they opened the show, they were looking for secondary people to sponsor it, like they usually do with big productions. That helped take a lot of the cost off of Disney itself. Let someone else foot the bill, but give Disney all the credit for it. Anyway, they brought it to the NBC executives, since they were the main sponsors at the time.

They just hated it. They hated everything that Bob had done, and they wanted to redo the entire thing. Not wanting to lose out on the money, Disney said fine. NBC scrapped the entire thing, and brought in Bob Finkel, who was a big-time producer. Finkel brought in Jackie Cooper as his assistant. You may remember Jackie from his acting career, as he was famous for playing Perry White in the *Superman* films in his later years.

So these two guys came in, and pretty much took over the entire show. The very first meeting we had with them, Jackie had a police whistle in his mouth. He'd blow the whistle when anything would get out of hand, to bring everybody back to attention. The two of them ran it like it was the Army! I got a big kick out of the fact that they kicked out Bob Jani; one crazy guy exchanged for these two even crazier ones.

Finkel came in one late Friday afternoon when we were laying out the final, full scale, sets. Even though it wasn't going to be an ice show, he decided he wanted the entire arena floor to look like ice. I couldn't believe it.

"When I come back Monday morning, that's what I want!"

I was in deep trouble. I didn't know what to do. I called some of my friends over at the Disneyland paint shop, and explained the situation. Thank God for all of them, because they really were like a family. When someone in the family asked for help, they all jumped right in.

A whole bunch of us worked all through the weekend to get it to look like ice. We'd sleep in shifts in the arena for a few hours, get up, and go back to work. I can't even tell you how long we worked for, but we got it done. I was thrilled.

Finkel came in Monday morning, and said that it looked fine. He didn't realize just what the hell we had to go through to make that happen for him to say it looked "fine."

The show itself was pretty successful. They did a couple of seasons of it, and they eventually had about four groups at once touring the show all over the world.

Crowd Enjoys Opening Of 'Disney on Parade'

By ROBERT McDOUGAL

From the moment Mary Poppins came swooping high above the wings flying high above the crowd to the last moment when crowds of eager children rushed out to surround Mickey Mouse, the opening night of "Disney On Parade" Wednesday held a packed house spellbound.

The show is celebrating the 50th anniversary of the founding of the Walt Disney empire which consists of cartoon and feature film production in addition to books, records and entertainment centers.

Performances continue tonight at 7:30. Saturday at 10:30 a.m., 2:30 and 7:30 p.m. and Sunday at 2 and 6 p.m.

An apt description of the presentation is flawless, but a description of the spectacle is spectacular. Costume design, lighting, choreography and execution of the spectacle were all without fault.

The show depends on a mixed media approach for its effect and on lavish costume and spectacular sound and props. A large screen is used to project animated settings and backgrounds, then at the appropriate time, the character comes alive on stage and continues the plot.

Early in the show, the story of Pinocchio on Pleasure Island uses the device to good effect.

story was perhaps a little too deep for the younger members of the audience whose attention seemed to wander, but only an occasional adult moved as a child prevailed on a parent to make a trip out for drinks and other necessaries.

The children were on the edge of their seats literally throughout the rest of the performance.

A hit with the children was a skit where two cars compete for the attention of Goofey. The scene ends in a high wire chase as Bug Herbie tries to force his attentions on the lovable hound in confrontation about 30 feet above the stage.

Most of the sound and music for the production came from a finely tuned Disney sound system, but is interestingly spiced with live music and sound effects which lend realism to the overall effect of the film, the actors and the music.

Act two was a Mary Poppins spectacular with a fleet of dancing chimney sweeps, and London's former social fabric in engaging and dancing. Mary enters and leaves by the aerial hoist system and appears to fly with the aid of her umbrella.

If your child has not seen one of the annual Disney productions, he should. If he has seen one before, the chances are that he has already persuaded you to go again this year.

Newspaper clipping about the opening of *Disney on Parade.*

IT'S KIND OF A CUTE STORY

This page: Shots from an old home movie of *Disney on Parade.*

Me in my office. Notice some of my own personal touches, along
with my artwork and photos of people that influenced me.

CHAPTER 14

SUPERVISING ART DIRECTOR AT DISNEYLAND

fter Walt passed away, Dick Irvine didn't know what to give me as an assignment. I was finishing up my Tomorrowland re-design work, and he definitely didn't want me back on the Haunted Mansion because he didn't like all the crazy Museum of the Weird ideas I had. Hell, it was pretty obvious that he didn't even want me in the building at that point. So, to get me out of his hair, he sent me off to Disneyland to be the Supervising Art Director.

Pretty much what that meant was, if they were changing the wallpaper in any of the buildings, it was my responsibility to pick out the wallpaper. If they were going to change the color of any of the buildings, it was my responsibility to pick out the color. If they were taking a curb out, I had to be down there to make sure that the curbs were taken out.

It was a lot of work, but it suited me pretty well. I did it for about three years, and I learned so much while there. There was a huge difference between working at WED and working directly in Disneyland every single day. It was absolutely an incredible education for me, because I was working with all the different divisions of the Park. That included janitorial, food, Maintenance, Operations and more. I really got to know the Park inside out and backwards. It was probably one of the greatest educations I've ever had because every division would tell me different stories, because most of them had people that had been working there since the Park opened. It was almost a history lesson for me to go through all that.

Back in those days, the Park was still closed on Mondays and Tuesdays. Both of those days were just filled with meetings with all the different divisions. I'd be going from one part of the Park to another all day long. I didn't have a bicycle or anything, so it got to be pretty tiring. Well, eventually I got permission to drive my car around Disneyland.

Yes, you read that correctly. I drove my beautiful little red Porsche around the Park. Crazy, right? It was marvelous, though. Their only requirement was that I had to keep a big piece of cardboard in the Porsche. Whenever I would park the car, I'd slide that piece of cardboard underneath it so the engine wouldn't drip oil onto the pavement. And no, I never parked in the Castle.

As Supervising Art Director, I sometimes had to give tours to outside folks, to show them how we did business at the Park. I would explain to them Walt's philosophies and how he did things. I used to tell them all about the different tricks he would use to help draw guests further into the Park and to move them along in their exploring.

One time, I was giving a tour to a group of Japanese business people. I was explaining to them how Walt put 'weenies' all over the Park to pull people from one place to another. In case you don't know what that is, a perfect example of a weenie is the Castle. You see it down the end of Main Street, and you're intrigued by it, so you walk closer to it to find out what it is. Walt used these all over the Park.

I was explaining this to the group, and this one Japanese lady says, "Mr. Crump, what's a weenie?"

Well, for us to explain it, it's pretty easy. A weenie is a hot dog. Walt was using the same trick that you did to dogs; dangle a weenie in front of their face to get them to do something. But in Japan, they just didn't know what it was. I had to go through this whole thing about the importance of a hot dog here in the United States, and how we call it a weenie. I'm not sure if she quite understood it after that.

We did a lot of interesting stuff during my time there, though. A lot of little changes that I'm pretty proud of. Hell, I personally changed every single light bulb in Bear Country during my three years as Supervising Art Director!

A good example of a small change that worked out well was the chains in the queues. We had some beautiful white chains around the queue for the Carrousel in Fantasyland. By the end of the day, though, those chains had been banged back and forth so much that they were all chipped. It always bothered me that the painters had to go out there every night to repaint them. I thought it was a waste of paint, and a waste of their time.

"Isn't there something that we can do about this, Rolly?" one of the painters asked me. I thought about it, and I came up with an idea.

"Why don't you see if there are any chains that we can purchase that are anodized aluminum?" He went out one day to travel to some stores to see what he could come up with. He

We designed this temporary backdrop for the Dixieland at Disneyland stage. Louis Armstrong liked it so much that he tried to take it home with him.

eventually came back with a sample of these old anodized aluminum chains that were gold. I took one look at them, and knew that was our solution. We bought a whole bunch, and changed out those chains that night. We had so many left over that we also changed out chains all over the rest of the Park, too, such as for Pirates of the Caribbean. That saved the painters a lot of time, and a lot of money.

We started using fiberglass in the Park for the same reason, actually. It helped cut down on the time and money spent on repairs. For example, there are these petrified wooden posts in Frontierland by the shooting gallery. They're just absolutely gorgeous, and fit into the theme really well. They were donated to Walt back in the 1950s by a gentleman in Montana. This guy was a collector of these wooden posts, and after he visited Disneyland, he knew he'd found a good home for them. He gave them to Walt and, sure enough, Walt liked them so much that he had them put into the Park.

Well, the thing about wood is that it rots. After about 20 years, these things started to really deteriorate. We took them out, but made some molds off of them. From those molds, we made fiberglass replicas. They look and feel exactly like real pieces of petrified wood. It was hard for a lot of folks to tell the difference, but they last forever, so they're still there. We even made some handrails out of them after that. You may have even run your hand along them once or twice, and didn't even notice.

Since that worked out so well in Frontierland, we started replacing other things with fiberglass versions all over the Park. Another great example is the lampposts on Main Street. Every night, Maintenance would come in and hose everything down to clean it. Obviously after a while, the lampposts would rust. We replaced those with fiberglass copies, along with all the lampposts in New Orleans Square. Next time you're around there, give them a knock or two. You'd never know it was fiberglass unless you heard that distinctive sound.

We did have a pretty big problem with wood rotting all over the Park, not just in Frontierland. One of the Maintenance guys came to me one day to ask about fixing up the building façades on Main Street, U.S.A. Every night, when the Park closed, they would wash down the buildings with water using pressurized hoses. Over the years, it started to really rot the wood. The Maintenance guy said the only thing holding them together was the paint!

Management wouldn't just agree to it, since it was a costly project, so we had to prove to them that it was necessary. We set up a meeting with all the Senior Vice Presidents of Disney so we could try to show them what exactly the problem was. They came down to Disneyland, and this Maintenance guy took an ice

IT'S KIND OF A CUTE STORY

The scale model of a new gift shop for Fantasyland.

The finished version of a new gift shop in Fantasyland.

pick to every building on Main Street. He would put the tip against the side of a building, and it would just slide into the wood with hardly any effort. It was like it was going into pudding! The point was proven, and Management approved the work order to repair the façades.

I also had this idea to add a little more detail to Pirates after it first opened. I always loved the scene with the city on fire. I just love how they created the effect to make it look like it was actually burning, too. It was another one of those simple things that worked out well.

They just used these clear sheets of Mylar, and set them at a 45 degree angle behind a window. They pointed some orange and red lights to reflect off them. When you turned on a fan, the Mylar would sway and wrinkle. That whole thing combined gave a pretty convincing fire effect.

I wanted to go a step further and pump the smell of charcoal into the room. You could get aerosol cans of any smell you wanted, and I thought we could place a few all around that scene to make it even more convincing. Management loved the idea, but they shot it down.

"If people smell it and think the place was really on fire, they're going to jump out of their boats and we're going to really have a problem," they told me. That one never got used, but I still think it would have been a fun thing to do.

Toward the back of Tomorrowland, there is a gorgeous palm tree called a reclinata. It's absolutely the most beautiful palm that you'll ever see. It turns out that is the largest palm of that style in the state of California. Bill Evans had seen this palm many years before in Santa Barbara.

When they were building Disneyland, he went to Walt and told him he wanted to buy that tree and put it somewhere in the Park.

"We'll do that one of these days," Walt told him. "I promise."

Bill kept on him about that for years, and Walt kept promising they would get it eventually. Eventually never came, though, and Walt passed away before they could buy it. A few days after Walt passed, Bill went and bought that tree himself for $3,000. He had it shipped directly to Disneyland.

Bill had been telling me about this palm for years, so he was excited to tell me he finally bought it.

"You have got to be here when we put in the ground," he told me. I asked him when they were doing it, and he said "Tomorrow morning at three o'clock!"

Being the Supervising Art Director, I pretty much had to be there when they put it in. I drove all the way down from Woodland Hills in the middle of the night to watch that palm being put into Disneyland. I didn't mind, though, because it meant something to Bill, and it meant something to me, too.

This is a really good example of how the people that worked for Disneyland really loved the Park, and thought the Park 'belonged' to them. I felt that way, too. After a while, the Park does belong to you. I felt like a King every Monday and Tuesday, walking around the empty Park, just taking it all in. It was absolutely special to me. That's why I think everybody took such great care of it back then. They loved it like it was their own. People would get upset if you started to change these little things about the Park that they loved, especially the people who worked there.

A good example of this was a coral tree that Bill Evans put in Adventureland way back when. One of the young guys from Operations, Bill Sullivan, came up to me and said he wanted to take it out.

"We could expand the queue line for the Jungle Cruise if that tree was gone," he told me. But I knew how much that tree meant to Bill.

"You're not going to take that tree out," I said. "There is no way. First of all, Bill Evans would kill you…" And that was pretty much all the explanation Sullivan needed. It's still there today, mainly because it's become part of Disneyland's landscape, and if you tried to remove it, Bill really would kill you.

There is one really good one that I always considered my own personal victory, because I snuck it past Management without them ever knowing. In Town Square of Main Street, U.S.A., by the flagpole, they had these ugly steel rods sticking out of the ground, with ropes connecting them, to keep people off the grass. They were ugly as hell, and looked out of place. I wanted to make something a little more pleasing to the eye, something that fit in more. I drew up a Victorian looking fence post, full scale, on a piece of cardboard.

I took that drawing and went directly to Maintenance with it. The proper way to do it was to fill out the paperwork, go through all the right channels, and if we were lucky, it would have been approved in a year. It would have cost a fortune, and I didn't want that. So I gave it to the guys, and within a few days, the first pieces of it were installed in the Park. No one questioned me about it, not even Management, because

A trash can near It's A Small World that I designed.

I knew to keep my mouth shut. I think those fences are still there today!

There were a few little things about the Park that always bothered me a lot early on, but I never had a chance to do anything about them. In fact, there are two really great stories about this.

The first one goes way back to when I was designing the façade for Small World. I designed all the lighting for what the façade would look like, being very aware that the ambient light coming from this big piece of architecture would pretty much illuminate the entire area. Well, the architect decided it needed two gigantic poles that were 60 feet in the air, with all these lights on them to flood the area with more light. It was like lighting a parking lot.

I went to Management, and said, "We're not going to put those damn things in there are we?" They assured me that they weren't, and not to worry about it. Next thing I know, we're finishing up the façade and here come these trucks with those gigantic lamp poles on them. I just had a fit! I went back to Management and they said, "Don't worry about it Rolly, we need them for security." I told them they didn't but they assured me they did.

It was a battle I wasn't going to win, so I had to just let it go. So now here I am, about 10 years later, and I'm in charge of making all these changes. I was walking through the Park one day, and Management came up to me and said, "You know those lights? They're horrible and they cost us a lot of money. We don't need them!"

I got a little smile on my face and said, "Well…cut the damn things down!" They were gone by the very next day. In the long run, I won that war! It was ten years later, but I still won.

The other story is also about lighting, but over in Tomorrowland. I remember when we re-designed it, I wasn't too happy with the company they brought in to do the lighting. It just looked ridiculous. They lit it about three times brighter than they should have. When you walked in Tomorrowland at night, there were no shadows because there was just too much damn light! It didn't give you a feeling of depth, and really threw the whole vibe off.

Finally, Management came to me while I was the Supervising Art Director and said, "Do you know what the electric bill is like for Tomorrowland?" I told them I had no idea.

"It's horrible! It's outrageous!" they said. "Can we take some out?"

I was thrilled about that. I said, "Yes! Take 50% out!" They did, and I saved the Company a hell of a lot of money. On top of that, I created a better atmosphere. To me, it's amazing that these simple little changes make so much of a difference in things. That's the stuff the guests really notice.

There was one electrician that I worked really well with during my time at Disneyland. Unfortunately, his name escapes me, but he had been there almost since the Park opened.

One evening, he and I were walking around the Park after hours near the entrance to Bear Country. It was really dark over there, and just seemed very out of theme with the rest of the area. I had an idea to help brighten it up a bit using a sloping hill off to the right hand side.

"We should get some lights up there in that embankment so people can see this area a little better," I said to the guy.

"You know, at one point, there were some lights there. I have no idea what happened to them," he replied.

He climbed over the fence that was around the hill, and started pulling debris away, and sure enough, the leaves began to glow from underneath. It turns out there were these fluorescent lights that were completely buried by all these dead leaves over the years.

We spent the rest of the night digging up about half a dozen lights.

This was an ongoing problem the landscaping department had with the electrical department. A lot of times, landscaping would start cutting the tree limbs and wind up cutting the wiring for the lights as well. I suppose at some point they decided to put these lights on the ground so the wires wouldn't continue to be cut. Eventually, when the leaves came down, they were covered up. Folks just forgot they were there, despite the fact that the lights stayed on all those years without anyone realizing it!

Well, now we had these six great big lights that, when uncovered, lit the area extremely well and solved our lighting problem.

Along the same lines, there was a walkway on the right hand side of the Castle that was incredibly dark. We were looking into putting lights there, but Management thought it would be too expensive. I had some of the guys look into how much a fountain would cost instead. My thought process was that if we put a fountain there, and lit it with just a few smaller lights, the light would bounce off the water and light the whole area. Of course, it was significantly cheaper, and the idea worked beautifully. We installed it and everyone, especially the money guys, was happy.

I themed the popcorn wagons around the Park as well, because I thought they were all pretty generic looking. They all had a Victorian look, regardless of where they were. I decided to make them more suited for their area so they would fit better. We even went as far as theming the little clowns turning the cranks to churn the popcorn in each cart. Those fellows were already there, but they got costume changes. The clown stayed for Main Street, but I changed it to a bear for Bear Country, a ghost for New Orleans Square and so on. Those little guys are still there today.

A stand I designed in Fantasyland as a place for artist Jess Rubio to do caricatures.

Because of all the different parts of the Park I worked in, I realized that I was really taking in a lot of information for just one person. There were all these groups that knew everything, but it was never funneled to one person. I realized there were beautiful stories there, so I started giving walks in the Park to people at WED. I'd get about a dozen at a time, start at the main gate, and take them through Disneyland. It would take me about an hour and a half to give them the history of the Park. That was something that I wanted to continue when I was still working for WED, but, of course, no one was really interested in it back then!

I loved working for Disney so much that I absorbed every possible thing that I could. I just love passing that on. And that's part of the reason why you're holding this book.

CHAPTER 15

WALT DISNEY WORLD

hen they decided to build Walt Disney World in Florida, they wanted to duplicate some of the dark rides in Fantasyland.

Dick Irvine called me up and said they were going to put me in charge of all the Fantasyland rides, and I was thrilled. I always loved the Disneyland dark rides, so I thought this would be a great time to try to improve on them a little bit. I came up with a list of the dark rides to bring over to Florida, and started to storyboard them out, leaving some things alone and coming up with some new ideas. As you may already know, one of those rides was Mr. Toad's Wild Ride. It was insanely popular at Disneyland at the time. So much so that Dick Nunis told me that he wanted to have TWO Mr. Toad rides at Walt Disney World.

"What do you mean by that?" I asked him.

"I want you to make two Mr. Toad rides, side by side, exactly the same." It was so popular that they wanted to make sure it had a high capacity in the Florida Park.

Well, I thought that was a dumb idea. Two rides, exactly the same? Why the hell would I do that for? I told him to let me think about it for a while, and I'd come up with something even better.

I went home that night to try to hash it out. What I came up with was eventually put into the Park. I had two Mr. Toad rides, but they were two completely different rides in the same building. The track layouts were completely different, which I thought was a great idea to throw people off. One on the left side and one on the right.

Both sides started in Toad Hall and took a look around in there. But then one of the cars would turn right and break through a wall, and the other would turn left and go through the pantry. From there, each side would have their own little adventure, and then come back together in the Town Square. They'd see each other again and almost get into an accident with each other before splitting off onto different adventures. Of course, both sides wound up in Hell at the end. I just thought it was an interesting idea to have the two sides be completely different, but intertwine with each other at certain parts of the ride.

It always made me laugh when a family went on the ride, and one half went on one side, and the other half went on the other, and they didn't realize both were different.

"Did you see the chickens?" "What? There were no chickens!" "What do you mean there were no chickens?" "Well, did you see the gypsy camp?" "What gypsy camp?"

I loved that ride. I really did. I was really proud of it. It was very popular when the Magic Kingdom opened, and it continued to be for a long time. Of course, as the years went on, Management wanted to put something new in there, and decided to take the ride out.

Believe it or not, there were people that protested about its closure. They had t-shirts and signs that said 'Save Mr. Toad' and 'Save Toad Hall' on it. It was really wild. They would walk around in front of the ride and chant and cheer. I was really touched by that.

I hoped that maybe, just maybe, their plan would work. Unfortunately, it didn't. It was gone by 1998. The original is still at Disneyland, which is good, but I'm still upset over the loss of my Toad.

I also really liked the Alice in Wonderland ride at Disneyland, so I wanted to do a variation of that

Opposite: **When Walt Disney World was built it was scaled up, causing it it lose the charm that Disneyland has.**

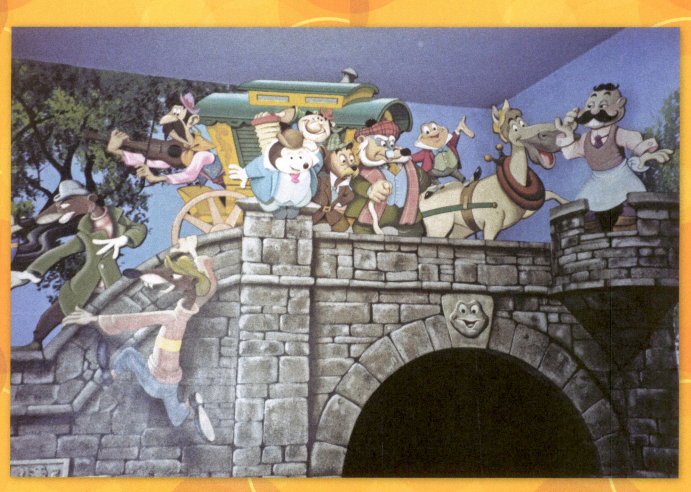

Above: The queue of Mr. Toad's Wild Ride, showing some of the characters you'd meet along your journey.
Below: Both sides of the ride ended with a quick jaunt through Hell.

IT'S KIND OF A CUTE STORY

Some more scenes from Mr. Toad's Wild Ride.

at Walt Disney World. Except, instead of being just a dark ride, I wanted to combine it with the Tea Cups to make it more interesting.

Alice goes to a tea party in the movie, so I thought it would be great if the ride vehicles were the Tea Cups. Just like the ones that spin at Disneyland, I wanted you to be able to spin them on the ride, too. That way, you'd be going through Wonderland, and you'd be able to spin around to see it from all angles. I always thought the movie was kind of crazy and wild, so I wanted to translate that into the ride. It would still have the same hourly capacity, which is what they were looking for, but it would have taken it to the next level where I thought it needed to be. It seemed to make a lot of sense to me, but not to Management. Obviously, they didn't do that, or build an Alice dark ride at all at Walt Disney World.

They eventually used that same idea for the Roger Rabbit ride at Disneyland, because both of those movies had the same kind of feel. The guy who did that ride 'borrowed' the idea from my old Alice design, and it turned out pretty good.

But I still think it would have been better in a Tea Cup.

When we were doing Walt Disney World, I'll be honest with you, I don't think Dick Irvine had a clue what he was doing. Without Walt's guiding hand, it was a bit of a mess. Don't get me wrong, Dick was a wonderful administrator, but as a designer he didn't know a thing.

At Disneyland, everything is scaled down. Nothing is the proper size. It's small, and that's what gives it part of its charm. It hugs you. Walt Disney World was all scaled up. Everything is larger than life, and they lost of lot of that charm in the process. For example, the Castle at Disneyland is only 77 feet tall. The one at Walt Disney World is 190 feet tall. That's a big difference.

When all of this work started taking place, I started getting a little perturbed about the fact that we were losing the look and style of Disney. Dick hired a lot of Art Directors and designers from 20th Century Fox to develop the Magic Kingdom. These were guys he worked with in the past, and he thought they would do a good job. But in the end, it just looked like a bunch of people tried to copy Disney.

There was a philosophy of design behind Disneyland. Everything had a good theme behind it, and I thought that was missing at Walt Disney World. A good example is the Enchanted Tiki Room. At Disneyland, we based our designs on the Sepik River regions of New Guinea. We used that as a template and we went from there. That was our philosophical theme behind it. When we were doing Walt Disney World, that philosophy was lost somewhere along the way.

That's not to say I dislike Walt Disney World. It's still a beautiful place, but it really got away from the vision Walt had to begin with. After I finished my projects, I bid the Company farewell for the second time. It just wasn't the same without Walt around anymore. His presence was sorely missed, not only on a personal level, but on a professional one as well.

I wasn't happy there any longer, so it was time to go off on my own again.

Exterior designs of the preview center that we designed.

CHAPTER 16

CiRCUS WORLD

rvin Feld, who was the President of Ringling Bros. and Barnum & Bailey Circus, got the idea to build a theme park based on the American circus. It was kind of a weird time for them, because they were still in a flux phase. Irvin used to own the whole thing, but sold it to Mattel in 1971 for fifty million dollars. They ran it for a few years, but by 1982, Irvin was in the middle of buying it back from them. So, this was right around that middle time, when he didn't quite fully own the whole thing yet, but he was going to again. Regardless, Mattel wanted to get this Circus World built so they were willing to foot the bill for it.

Irvin hired an architect to design this Circus World theme park for him. The guy he hired was a good architect but he designed all the components of Circus World like a World's Fair pavilion. There was nothing there that looked anything like a circus. It was just a lot of big, blocky buildings.

Irvin was not really happy with the design, because it was not what he had in mind. Eventually, he had hired a guy that I had worked with at Disneyland. This guy worked in Operations, which is what Irvin was going for. He thought that if he got some folks who worked at Disney, and already knew the ropes about how to run a theme park, it would run a hell of a lot smoother. This guy told Irvin all about me, that I was quite a designer, and had worked directly with Walt.

Irvin was convinced I was the guy for the job, and he contacted me to see if I would be interested in drawing up a master plan for Circus World. The idea really intrigued me, so I told him I'd love to.

Scale model of the layout for Circus World.

I started to do my research and I found out all sorts of interesting tidbits about the circus. I learned that the idea of a circus was actually invented in the United States. A lot of people, including myself, thought that the circus was created over in Europe. The Ringling Brothers were the ones who really brought it to the mainstream. They were just a bunch of crazy brothers doing some crazy stuff. They hired a lot of entertainers from Europe, though, so that's probably where that line of thought came from. They would go on the road with this show and they eventually became this big thing.

I realized that in order to do a theme park about circuses, it should be designed like it was around the turn-of-the-century, which was the height of their popularity. Everything had to have a sort of period feel to it. I'm talking about architecture, the costumes, the graphics; everything should look like it was straight from the 1900s, because that is when circuses were so popular.

I was in charge of Design 27 at the time, so we designed and built a model for the whole thing. We had a lot of illustrations and mock-ups for posters, and it all really impressed Irvin. He loved it so much that he asked us to design everything else in the park, too. So we did.

We really designed it to be like you were visiting a circus of the old days. There would be a big top with an actual, permanent circus in it so you could see the show. But there would have been a ton of other things to do as well. We had dark rides that were based on Tom Thumb (one of the sideshow performers) and a dark ride based on clowns. We also put in a clown college, to get people to experience what it was like to be a clown.

We had it set up so it would be like a circus town, in a way. You know when a circus comes into town, they have the part everybody sees, but in the back, behind all the hustle and bustle, is the mini town the performers would set up to live in for the week they were there. We made that part of the park, and wanted people to walk around there to feel like they were part of the show. The performers would have walked around the town, going about their business, and also doing some crazy tricks. A guy would be training his eagle. Another one would be balancing a wheelbarrow on his chin. Hell, there would have even been someone walking a wire above their head!

We incorporated all of the slang that the circus performers used to lend some authenticity to it. For example, instead of a restaurant, we had a cookhouse, because that is what they would call it. The cookhouse would put up a little flag that said "Hotel" on it when they were open for business, and the performers would know where to go to eat. We never did find out why they put up that little flag, but we did it, too. If you were going to go to the bathroom, you were going to the donniker. All of the restrooms had a sign that said 'donniker' on them. We really did want it as authentic as possible.

When it was all done and planned out, Irvin came to me and asked me to move to Florida to help build the thing.

"If all you guys move to Florida, whatever team you had put this plan together, I'll double their regular salary." That sounded like a pretty good deal to me! I went to all the kids that worked for me, of which there was about six at the time, and told them the deal. Most of them agreed, but a couple of the gals were

Turn-of-the-century clown signage at Circus World.

The cookhouse, where you could grab a bite to eat.

IT'S KIND OF A CUTE STORY

married and couldn't leave their families behind. One of the other girls, though, was the breadwinner in the family, so she dragged her husband along. So we packed up all the furniture in the office, and got ready to move down to Florida. The greatest part of all was the truck that picked all of our furniture up also had an elephant in it!

By the time the truck got to Texas, the elephant went berserk for some reason. He tore the whole moving van apart. It was a mess. When they got to Florida, about half of what we had in that truck was completely destroyed. Ringling Brothers had to pay all of us for our damaged possessions. That should have given me a clue as to what I was getting myself into for the next year but, at the time, I just took it all in stride.

I had them build a preview center with an IMAX film to promote the place while we were getting it done. I had them build it in this weird oval shape, and then put a roof over it. Then I had a striped canvas put over the top of the whole thing to make it look like a circus tent. The sides were painted in big white and red stripes so, when you would drive by, you'd do a double take to make sure you really saw this circus tent standing there. It looked great.

About this time, Mattel had gotten into financial problems and they couldn't afford to build Circus World anymore. Irvin really believed in the project, though, and started going around to different companies to try to get financing.

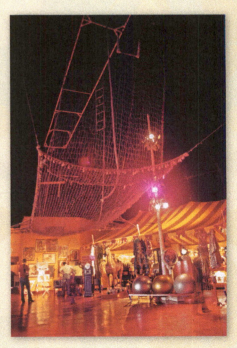

Most of our designs for Circus World harkened back to the turn-of-the-century feel of a circus.

He would fly us out with him to give a presentation on what Circus World was going to be. Shell Oil was interested at one time and ready to throw their money into it. But then we had a gasoline crunch, which was just terrible. The government saw that Shell was going to invest in building this theme park and put a stop to that right away. They felt that any money that Shell had should be used to help keep the economy stable and keep oil at a reasonable price. After going around for three months trying to sell it, it just wasn't working. Meanwhile, that preview center we'd built had expanded, and now offered camel rides, elephant rides and a few other assorted things.

By that time, it wasn't going to be a theme park anymore. Irvin called us in to tell us and basically said, "I'm sorry." We thought we were going to be in Florida for five years, designing and building this thing. But a year had come and gone, and it was now dead in the water. We all went home to California, kind of defeated. A scaled down version of the park was eventually built a few years later, though most of the work my team did was thrown out the window.

Entrance ticket for Circus World.

The preview center which was set up like an actual circus.

Crafty Coyote relaxing after enjoying the spoils of his thievery.

CHAPTER 17

KNOTT'S BEAR-Y TALES AT KNOTT'S BERRY FARM

 think it was September of 1974, right after I was finishing up work on Circus World, when Knott's Berry Farm approached me about doing a dark ride for them. They'd heard I was coming back to California and wanted to get in touch with me.

The fellow that contacted me was an accountant named Dick. He had worked for Disney, where he knew me from, then went on to become at Vice President at Knott's. He and Marion Knott, who owned the park, decided that they wanted to do a dark ride for their new area of the park. Dick told Marion that I was no longer with Disney and suggested they contact me to do it. When I flew back from Florida, I went to meet with them.

When the ride opened later on, the area was themed as the Roaring 20's, but it wasn't like that when we started it. Wally Huntoon, a designer for Knott's, had this idea that the dark ride would take place inside a gypsy camp. When I went to meet with them, Marion gave me the script Wally had written for it. It was a cute little story about a young boy and his donkey going off to the fair, and they have all these adventures that they run into along the way. It was just a bare bones outline, so I began to embellish it. I didn't know much about the area they were putting it in, other than the fact that there was a huge show building they were going to put it in. So, like I said, it started off being a gypsy ride. Later, they decided to develop it into a much larger area. At the last minute, though, they decided to call the area the Roaring 20's! So, it was definitely an evolution from start to finish.

But, before all that happened, I had to make a presentation to the Knott family of what I thought the ride should be. Walter Knott was still alive at that time, so I gave the whole presentation to the entire family: him, Marion, her brother, her two sisters and their husbands. I did a lot of story ideas, sketches, and layouts for it, and really sold my ideas to them. They liked it, so they decided to give me the green light.

I have to say that I was really honored to work with Knott's on the ride. I especially enjoyed working with Marion. Knott's had really built an incredible park over the years. Walt Disney used to go to Knott's Berry Farm all the time, and he got a lot of his ideas for Disneyland from their park. I was very excited to work for them because I had

My original notes on how I wanted to lay out the ride.

Overhead view of how the ride was laid out, as drawn by me.

grown up with Knott's since I was 9 years old! I remember when it really was a farm. I even remember before the Ghost Town was put in, when my grandfather would take us down there for the chicken dinner and boysenberry pie. So, when I met Marion, we got to be real close friends and she told me some interesting stories about when she was a little girl. She told me her Dad would make her stand out by the road, holding a stalk of rhubarb, and waving it at all the people going by to entice them in!

Once I got the okay, that's when I contacted an old friend of mine, named Tommy O'Neil. He owned a company called Fantasy Fair, which did all the animated window displays for Disneyland back in the 1960s and 1970s. Every time Disney would release an animated feature, they would hire Tommy to dress the windows with little animated displays to help promote it. I knew that he had a good understanding of fantasy and that he had a certain knowledge of mechanical devices, so I thought he was just the man for the job. So, I went down to see him and told him all about the project.

"I've got this great opportunity to design a dark ride for Knott's Berry Farm. Would you like to build it?" I asked him. He was a little surprised, because he'd only done little displays like at Disneyland. That's what his company was known for.

"No, I'm serious!" I told him. "I'll design it and lay it out for you, but I want you to build it!"

"Oh my God," he said to me. "This is a huge undertaking. I'll have to go home and think about it. Come see me tomorrow." I went to see him the next day, and he told me he'd went home the night before with a huge headache and just went to bed. He didn't know what to do because it was such a big job! But, eventually he agreed.

We started developing it right away. It was kind of interesting because when we first looked at what we were going to do, I just took him through the ideas. I talked him through it, but didn't show him any sketches or layouts. I told him we needed to put a budget together to let Knott's know how much it would cost to install. Well, Tommy immediately went home again with a migraine headache!

He called me back the next day and said, "Well, I think I've worked out a good number. I think it looks like $600,000." But I thought about it and said, "No, Tommy, I think it's more like $900,000." I had a better idea of the cost since I was used to working with Disney and their budgets. So, we decided to set the budget at $900,000. But even that was a low figure for a ride, especially back then.

We decided that the idea of going to a gypsy fair was still a really fun concept, so we stuck with that. Originally, all my sketches were of humans doing this. You would meet various gypsies here and there along the way. During this time, we came up with the idea of the Frog Forest, and the Fortune Teller Camp. Some of the sketches I had done showed the gypsies dancing with bears and everybody really liked the bears! The

IT'S KIND OF A CUTE STORY

idea was kicked around that maybe we should replace all the humans with bears.

So, Knott's brought in an outside marketing firm to test it and find out if the public liked the idea. I didn't really agree with them bringing in the outside firm, because I was so used to Walt's philosophy of doing things. He never test marketed anything. If he felt something was a good idea, he just went ahead and did it.

But they brought some people in, and showed them the artwork. Based on those tests, they decided using bears was a good idea. I mean, everybody really liked the animals! So my initial idea evolved, like I mentioned earlier, into a show with animals standing in for humans. That's when we came up with the idea of the 'Knottsenbear-y' family being part of the ride.

The Knottsenbear-y family bid you goodbye.

Original concept sketch for the Factory and the Chug-A-Chug machine.

That's where the Factory scene came in, with the juices, jams and all that.

That's when we put in the Chug-A-Chug machine, which my son Chris built. I knew that he was an excellent carpenter, and he would do a wonderful job. He understood how to work with me, which was a huge help. I'd just give him a sketch, and he'd build these marvelous things just from that. Steve Kirk did the little model of the Chug-A-Chug, and with that tiny model, Chris built this great machine. In fact, it was the biggest piece of animation in the entire ride.

After you passed the Chug-A-Chug, you went into Frog Forest and to the Fortune Tellers. Then you went down the tube into the Weird Woods, before all the characters came together at the Fair.

A lot of people used to ask me about that steep decline in the Spider Tunnel that took you to Weird Woods. That was designed because, in the original concept, there was going to be a free fall there. The cars would climb to the top of that hill, and then it was supposed to be released like a roller coaster. There were talks with Arrow Development, the folks responsible for a lot of the Disney rides, but eventually we went with someone else who was a lot cheaper. Of course, being cheaper meant we had to take out that free fall, but it was a good compromise.

We were originally just going to make that part all black, like you dropped down a black hole all of a sudden. All that rockwork was done with Pyre-Cure paper. It's what they use for insulation on roofs, and it is flameproof. On the back, it's shiny, like tin foil. It also has all kinds of soft mesh wire in it, so you can shape it anyway you want, and it'll hold that form. That's how we made our rockwork very inexpensively. It was like you were in this crinkled, shiny cave, and to make it even more surreal, we shot off strobe lights in there. It gave the whole thing this really weird effect, but I thought it looked pretty good. My goal was to kind of screw up people's eyes with it, so when you hit the Weird Woods, everything would look even weirder because your

My original concept sketch for Zaz in the gypsy camp.

IT'S KIND OF A CUTE STORY

eyes were all messed up. It was a simple, yet effective, effect.

While we were speaking to Arrow about building the ride, the vehicles that they had Dave Rudderow design were made to look like streetcars. They were nice and everything, but he wanted to put a top on them. I was against the idea, though, because I thought if you put a top on it, you'd be blocking out a lot of the stuff we were trying to achieve visually. I made him take the tops off them, but it was still basically a streetcar design. That's why there was a little headlight in front of each car.

There are a couple things I was particularly proud of on that ride. For example, the berry smell in the Factory was always one of my favorites. I got that idea from the Timber Mountain Log Ride at Knott's. Every time you went through the flume, you could smell pine trees. I always thought you smelled the real trees, but they told me they sprayed the smell in with aerosol cans. I thought it would be great to get the smell of sweet berries during the Factory sequence, and we made that happen. It was a nice little touch.

Another thing was when we mixed black light with incandescent light. That was something I always wanted to try while working at Disney, but Management believed that if it was a dark ride, it should only be UV lighting. I always thought you could get much more of a fantasy feel if you mixed the two, but Disney never really let me explore that option.

I got the idea for that from the Movieland Wax Museum in Buena Park, California, in the early 1960s. They had this Count Dracula lying in his coffin, and, of course, they used incandescent lighting in the whole place. But where he was lying in the coffin, they had black light shining right on him, giving him this really eerie look. I stood there, looking at this combination, and thought it looked really great.

Now that I had the chance, I was definitely going to give it a shot on Bear-y Tales. I thought it would help people get accustomed to the light inside the ride faster. When you're standing in line for a dark ride, you're usually out in the sun. Once you're on the ride, your eyes don't have a chance to open up and adjust right away. So, for the first 30 seconds or so, you're missing out while your eyes are still trying to get used to the dark. Some dark rides are only 90 seconds long, so that's an awful lot to miss out on.

What I decided to do was put incandescent lighting in the Factory so it was close to the sun outside, and help people's eyes adjust. When you got to Frog Forest, I went to black light. I still used incandescent light on the water, though, because water doesn't sparkle very well under UV lighting. The Fortune Teller Camp and the Weird Woods were also completely black light to give them much odder feeling. The Fair itself was half and half. All the backgrounds and foliage used black light, but we put incandescent on the characters. I thought it turned out extremely successful.

Tommy had started production of the characters and sets already. It was really in full swing. But then Marion came in and said, "Well…maybe I'd like this to be a Western ride instead."

All of a sudden, I had to start redrawing the characters like cowboys! We spent a few weeks doing that, redressing sets to be like the old West, and changing the Factory into a gold mine. I barely got some cowboy hats on some frogs, when she decided to go back with the original gypsy idea.

In the end, though, Marion finally decided to go with the Roaring 20's theme. That's why, in the finale, they've all got straw hats and such. But it worked because we stayed with the fantasy aspect of it. It really was like looking at a children's book, and all the animals you encountered were just the type you would meet on the way to the fair. Even though she kept changing her mind, we just went ahead with building the characters once we got going. It was simple enough to swap out the clothing for whatever new style Marion came up with next.

I ended up doing a caricature of Marion that I gave her when we were all done with the ride. I designed her so that she was part gypsy, part cowboy and part Roaring 20's. I even had her waving a stalk of rhubarb! I also drew in some Chinese designs on her, and I wrote, "We've been through gypsies, cowboys and Roaring 20's…before you're finished, I'm sure you'll want to make this a Chinese ride!" She took it in good stride, though, and had it hanging up in her office for a while!

For those of you who remember, the ride was on the second level. A lot of people ask me about why that was, and the simple answer is that's the space that was given to us. They didn't really have a reason for it; they just decided that's where the ride was going to go. That's where the gypsy camp was originally, but they moved all that downstairs. We still had a pretty good sized area. It was somewhere close to 20,000 feet,

Original concept sketch for the gypsy camp.

which is fairly big for a ride.

    The mural in the load area that people remember so fondly was done by Suzie McLean. We sat down together to come up with it, and used the same formula that Disney used on their dark rides to design it. The idea was that the mural showed the story of what's going to happen to you once you got on the ride. It was a huge wall to cover, but Suzie did a magnificent job on it. She's an incredible designer.

    I actually got her to come work with me at Design 27 when she was still in high school! She had been dating my partner's son at the time when he mentioned her being an artist to me. I thought, "Oh boy…" I

Doctor Fox hawking his wares.

thought he was just trying to get in his son's good graces. When they brought her over, I had her do a few sketches, and I was really blown away. I hired her in on a part-time basis, and then finally full-time in 1971.

    I was lucky she was still with me at the time Knott's came about, because her mural really gave people a great first impression of the ride. She also did all the wanted posters for Crafty Coyote, as well as laying out all the signs in the ride, too. After she left us, she got a job at WED as a graphics designer for a while.

    The ride opened on July 4th, 1975, after about 6 months of work. I thought we did an amazing job in that short amount of time, especially considering the fire damage we had to repair.

The show building shortly after a fire destroyed most of it.

For those of you who don't know about that, Tommy O'Neil had a non-Union shop. He wisely thought that it wouldn't be a good idea for them to start installing the characters in the show building until the Union folks were done doing what they had to do in there. Knott's had hired a Union contractor to build the building itself, but they said that it would be okay and we shouldn't worry about it.

Well, we installed about 50% of the ride, when all of a sudden one night, it just went up in flames. The fire department put it out, but everything was just a mess. They brought in an investigator who determined that it was a professional job. The fire had started in five places at the same time, so they thought the Union guys were behind it. All our hard work just went up in flames, and that was very sad.

We didn't have a lot of time before the ride opened at that point. I believe we got a 6 week extension for it, but that's about it! It took Chris 3 months to build the Chug-A-Chug machine the first time around, but to meet the deadline, he did the second one in only 6 weeks! So it was definitely an interesting and challenging time frame. I mean, not only did we design the whole thing, but we installed it, too. We worked night and day, usually until 2 or 3 in the morning, to make sure it was done. We'd get a bunch of six-packs and hamburgers, and have our own little parties in the ride every night.

But we finished on time, and they threw a magnificent opening night reception for the whole Roaring 20's area. The food was wonderful, and I really believe that Knott's has the best food in the world. It was a great party. Bear-y Tales was something we all really enjoyed, despite its challenges.

For about 6 weeks after the ride opened, I went down every other night at around 3 o'clock in the morning, and worked with the Maintenance crew to correct little things to help keep the ride going. It was kind of funny, because one night they put a ladder in one of the cars. I think someone left it there accidental-

ly, but they thought it would be funny to turn the ride on, and let the ladder go through it! The car made a sudden turn, and the ladder got stuck. It went right through some of the sets and jammed the ride! It was a mess, but we managed to fix it all before morning.

The bottom line is that it was a wonderful project, and I really enjoyed doing it. The folks who worked with me loved doing it, too. The best part is that people still come up to me today and tell me how much they loved that ride. In fact, it's the one I get the most compliments about. That always makes me feel good!

Inside the Factory, guests travel past the Chug-A-Chug machine.

Imagineering

November 5, 1982

Dear Rolly:

I just want you to know how much I appreciate your leadership role in creating The Land pavilion for Epcot Center.

It is a marvelous place, full of good cheer, good food, good fun and especially entertainment and learning experiences.

Please let me know when you will have a chance to visit Epcot Center so that we can make some special arrangements for you.

Sincerely,

Martin A. Sklar
Vice President
Creative Development

MAS:tv

cc: Carl Bongirno
     Orlando Ferrante
     Pat Scanlon

WED ENTERPRISES • Glendale, California/Lake Buena Vista, Florida   HEADQUARTERS • 1401 Flower Street, Glendale, California 91201 • 956-6500

LAKE BUENA VISTA OFFICE • P.O. Box 40, Lake Buena Vista, Florida 32830 • 828-2271

im•ag•i•neer'ing.' Imaginative Concepts in Design, Architecture, Engineering and Entertainment. – See Disneyland in California and Walt Disney World in Florida

A letter sent by Marty Sklar, thanking me for my work on EPCOT.

CHAPTER 18

Back at Disney

hen EPCOT started to really move forward years after Walt's passing, Disney asked me to come back to help work on it. We were never going to be able to achieve Walt's original vision, but we were definitely trying to do something that would have made him proud.

John Hench had been working on the master plan of EPCOT for three years, and hadn't come up with anything yet. So Marty Sklar, who was in charge, called me in, and asked if I would mind taking a crack at it.

I got one of the architects I worked with often, and we did a master plan of what I thought EPCOT should be. World Showcase wasn't one big pond of water in my version. It was a series of islands, and you had to take a boat to China. Then from China, you might have to take a carriage over to India, and so on. It was all very mysterious in my eyes. You couldn't see what was back there, because it was all nestled in little valleys and hills, hidden away. I thought World Showcase should be intriguing.

We had a Tower of Spaceship Earth, right in the center of it all. There was an observation deck on it, letting you see the entire Park. We had the monorail drop you off in the center of EPCOT, too. There was also a one-way system that would pick you up when you got off of the monorail. We had the whole transportation system worked out. In fact, we had the transportation pavilion, which was sponsored by General Motors, right by the pond of water. All the boats would leave from the General Motors transportation pavilion for the various countries. All of the transportation methods to, from, and around EPCOT would go in and out of that pavilion. I mean, it only made sense because it was the transportation pavilion.

When we had a meeting with all the Vice Presidents, John didn't know that Marty had asked me to do that. So when Marty said I was going to show my master plan for EPCOT, it didn't sit too well with John. He was about ready to go up in flames, because he was furious they had asked me to do a master plan.

I stood up and I started giving my presentation, but John stood up with me and started screaming because he was so mad.

"Jesus Christ, Roland," he says. "You've been with this Company for over 25 years and you haven't learned a God damned thing!" He came right out and said that my design was a piece of crap.

"John, it may not be perfect, but yours is far worse." I told him. "You've got a pond of water out there that's got a bunch of condominiums around it, and you're telling me that they are different parts of the world?" I didn't like the idea of these 'show buildings' he had come up with that would house different countries inside of them.

He and I started really going at it. It's funny, because no one ever really stood up against John. I mean, he was John Hench, he was really something. But once I had an idea in my head, I would defend it to the death, especially if I thought it was something Walt would have liked. All the Vice Presidents were about ready to crawl under the table until one of them started laughing and clapping. He even started chanting, "Go John, go John!"

"I've never seen this much life in you before!" he told John, right in the middle of us going at it. It was kind of funny. After that was over with, I was never asked to work on the EPCOT master plan again. John said he would have a new master plan in a week, and that was that.

The original Wonders of Life pavilion was pretty different than the one EPCOT wound up with. It was supposed to be called the Life and Health pavilion. We designed it so it was all about healthy living, and we recruited the best health educator in the United States on as a consultant. His name was Dr. Charles Lewis and he worked at UCLA. I used to call him Dr. Chuck and he got a kick out of that. He had the greatest dry sense of humor of anyone I've met, and because of that, we got along just fine.

He came up with the best line I've ever heard that sort of became our motto for the pavilion and, eventually, the rest of EPCOT: "If it's a ton of fun, and an ounce of information, you'll reach the teachable moment." As soon as I heard it, I thought, 'This is what EPCOT should be about.'

We worked on that place for almost a year, because we realized that health educators do nothing but argue. Some would say eggs are good for you, while others would say you should never eat eggs. We went to a health conference, and we listened to all these different people argue with each other about the health laws. We were trying to put together a pavilion that would appease all these people but it was hard when no one could agree on anything!

I finally was getting fed up with it, so I went to Dr. Chuck and asked, "Isn't there a common denominator that all of these health educators will say they agree on?"

"Oh yes," he said. "The eight health habits."

"What in the hell are the eight health habits?" I had no idea, but I needed to know so we could get the ball rolling.

"You know, they're sleep, diet, exercise…all those things. Nobody will argue with any of that!"

So I took those eight health habits, and I created the Great Midway of Life. I designed it so it was like one of those old time midways you'd find on a pier somewhere. There was a show in there about all the health habits. Right in the center of it all was Care-of-Self Carousel, which had all of the health habits represented as little tin figures. We also had a ride-through of the human body.

Yes, that does sound similar to what they had when the pavilion finally opened, but that's not how I designed it. What you got was a motion simulator, Body Wars, which I didn't like too much. My idea was pretty different. It was the same type of concept, though. You're reduced to a small size, and you take a journey through the entire human body, but my version was sort of a smooth roller coaster in a way, backed by a classical music soundtrack.

It would take you through all these different organs, while we had a voice coming through, telling you exactly where you were. I wanted everything to be anatomically correct in the visuals, along with the sounds. I wanted it to look and sound like you were actually there. You'd slowly work your way up to the top of the head, and get released into a brainstorm. I did find out from one of our consultants that we really do have brainstorms, and that's where the little roller coaster part would come into play. It was a neat little idea.

There was also an interactive portion we called the 'You Bet Your Life Gambling Hall.' It had a shooting gallery with a few games emphasizing different aspects of health and fitness. One of which had these little tin toys along the top that showed people doing various activities, such as running, swimming, riding a bicycle, and so on.

Underneath all of these tin toys were different types of food that you could shoot, like an apple, a sandwich or a piece of cake. When you shot one of the foods, a computer screen in front of you would tell you how many calories were in it, and how long it would take to burn them off while doing each particular activity. So, you would shoot the apple, and it would say it was 20 calories, and it would take an hour of swimming to burn it off. When you shot the cake, it would tell you how many calories it was, and that it would take 3 days of swimming to get rid of it. It was a neat little idea, and pretty ahead of its time for 1978.

We built a model of the whole thing for Management to look over. This was about the time they leased space in New York, in the RCA Building. They set out all the models for the different pavilions, trying to secure corporate sponsorships. We figured our pavilion would cost about $60 million, so we were asking for $30 million in sponsorship, and Disney would put up the other half. It's amazing, because they spent so much money just trying to get these sponsorships to begin with. With the model in New York, they'd fly me there on a Sunday evening. They would put me up at the Waldorf Astoria for the night, I'd do the presentation Monday morning, and then fly back Monday afternoon. This happened quite a few times!

One of the best presentations I gave was to the President of Pfizer. He absolutely loved it. He told me that they would love to do it, but the problem was that all of their money was in Ireland. I had no idea what the hell that even meant! Evidently, their financial package, which is where they had their money, was in Ireland. For whatever reason, they couldn't just get that money for the sponsorship. If it wasn't for that, he told me, he would definitely do it.

We just couldn't find a sponsor for it. It was supposed to be an opening day pavilion, but we just couldn't get the money. Eventually, long after I left the project, MetLife came in to sponsor it. It was given to another project manager to design, and it didn't open until 1989.

My team and I were also going to do the General Electric pavilion, before it became Horizons. I think we worked for about 3 months on it. We had Thomas Edison serving as an Audio-Animatronic Master of Ceremonies for the entire thing. For our preshow, we had something called T&E, designed by Scott Hennesy and Stevie Kirk, two of the young Imagineers working with me. T&E stood for the process you go through to make something work, trial and error. We had these cavemen doing some trial and error, where they eventually invented the umbrella, and it became the 'parasol of progress.' In my opinion, it was the funniest damn show that was ever put together.

The main show had Thomas Edison talking about all sorts of stuff. We also had a little village, where you went into the different buildings. Inside each one, there was someone that would talk to you about percentages, dollars and cents, and better living through General Electric. We basically took all the information they gave us, and created these beautiful little shows around them. Marty Sklar and John Hench would not let us show it to General Electric, though. In fact, we came up with three different shows, and they made us throw all of them out the window. We were never allowed to present them to General Electric's top management, so obviously, they never got built either.

It was fun, though, because we had Stan Freberg help us out a bit on that one. Stan was a famous voice actor and comedian, but he was also a brilliant advertising creative director. I think he was one of the funniest men ever put on this Earth.

He was fun to work with, and had some pretty bizarre ideas for the pavilion. One of them was that he thought it would be neat to design the pavilion to look like a box that light bulbs come in, with the light bulbs sticking out of it. He also thought that people shouldn't wait in line to see the attraction, but rather be herded into moving carts. Inside each cart would be a TV that would entertain you as you waited, almost making the line a ride in itself. I remember when he pitched all of this to Marty and John, he came out feeling really good about it.

I turned to him and said, "I hate to tell you this, but they're not going to build anything that you've designed."

"Well, why not?!" he asked.

"Just trust me," I told him. And sure enough, they weren't going to. When he found out, he just stood up and left the building, and never came back.

I ended up designing The Land pavilion, too. Kraft told us that if we did a pavilion on food, they would give us $30 million if we would put up the other $30 million, so that's how that came about.

Claude Coats laid out the original idea for The Land pavilion. When the first group of Kraft executives came in for our presentation on it, Claude just sort of fumbled and mumbled during the meeting. He did a walkthrough of the entire thing for them, and he mumbled his way through it. It was kind of atrocious, honestly. He had no presence whatsoever. So Marty Sklar came up to me afterward, and said, "Tomorrow Rolly, you give the show."

The next day, I gave the new batch of executives the presentation. What happened was they wanted to have a presence in EPCOT so badly that they'd planned on buying it whether somebody mumbled through the presentation or not! So, we were given the go-ahead.

I started working with some folks from the University of Arizona who were studying hydroponics. That's when you grow plants using mineral nutrient solutions, in water, without soil. It was interesting to me, because they were trying to figure out how to grow tomatoes in outer space.

Carl Hodges was the guy from the University of Arizona I worked with mainly. He was just a brilliant guy, and really taught me a lot about horticulture. We were working on the main attraction for the pavilion, and decided to do the whole ride with live plants. Well, John Hench just had a fit about that.

Me pointing out some of the finer points on the model of The Land pavilion to fellow Imagineers Jeff Burke (right) and Doris Hardoon (left).

"You can't put live plants in a building, they won't survive!" he was yelling at me.

"This is hydroponics, John," I told him. "They'll survive just fine. That's the whole point of this pavilion." But he kept insisting that it couldn't be live plants, and there had to be fake foliage. Luckily, with Carl backing me up, Marty eventually agreed with me, and shot down Hench's idea.

I went out to Tucson, Arizona where I spent a lot of time with Carl in the greenhouses where he was growing all these hydroponic plants. It was just amazing to learn all these new things, and then go back and apply it to the Listen to the Land attraction. Carl and I laid out where every single plant should go in that ride. I think Carl and his hydroponics kind of took The Land up to the next level. He really helped make it a success. It was really the only EPCOT pavilion actually doing the work that would help us in the future. It wasn't just some ride telling you about the stuff that could be coming soon. You learned about the future advances, and then you got to see it happen right in front of you. I was really thrilled about the ride. It always made me laugh that you could go through the ride to see tilapia in their tanks, swimming around, and then you can go upstairs and eat one of those same tilapia.

Kitchen Kabaret was a really cute Audio-Animatronic show that we did for The Land which advocated healthy eating. It helps illustrate a point I always make, that you really have to believe in the people that work for you and just turn them loose. I'm a big believer in that. You get a much better end product when you're not just some dictator to your team. Let them be creative, and explore stuff that may or may not work.

I remember the characters that were in Kitchen Kabaret were some pretty original and stylized creations. Everything was in the middle of getting sculpted when I got a call from one of my guys telling me that John Hench wanted us to re-design all the characters. I went down there, and found John ranting and raving, saying that what we did were not the typical Disney characters. He wanted us to have Disney-type characters in the show, otherwise he felt it wasn't going to be successful. He was talking about the kind everyone was used to, with 3 stripes on the white gloves and so on.

IT'S KIND OF A CUTE STORY

I listened to John rant and rave for a while about that, and blow off some steam. When he started winding down, I said, very calmly, "John, let me ask you something. Wasn't there an Academy Award that Disney won one time that didn't feature ANY Disney-type characters, called *Toot, Whistle, Plunk and Boom*?"

John stared at me for a second, and then just turned around and walked away. I broke his entire rant right there, because you have to remember something doesn't always have to look like Mickey Mouse to work out for the best.

When Nestlé took over sponsorship of The Land, they didn't want Kitchen Kabaret there anymore. They wanted a new show. I got Jim Steinmeyer, another Imagineer, to help me out on this one. We thought it would be neat to have the different fruits become caricatures of popular musicians and play parodies of their songs. We thought of some good rock songs, and came up with new lyrics that had to do with nutrition and eating healthy.

We both loved The Beach Boys, especially the song *Good Vibrations*, so we knew we had to get them in there. We turned that into *Good Nutrition*, sung by The Peach Boys. Once we got that done, the rest of the songs just came naturally. Jim did a wonderful job of writing all of the new lyrics. Since we were using rock songs, we thought Food Rocks would be a great name for the show. Especially since we were turning all of these foods into rock and roll bands, we thought it just fit well.

We had to contact all the recording companies to get their approval to use the songs, though. It had to go through legal, which we thought was going to be a nightmare, but luckily they loved the idea and they went ahead with contacting everyone about it. A lot of folks said, "Yeah, fine, go ahead and do it," but some of them said, "This is a great idea. We'll even record the songs for you!" I thought that was pretty neat.

There happened to be a woman who worked in the lighting department that used to do rock shows. She was assigned to work with us on lighting our show. When we sat down to talk about it, she started asking us all sorts of questions about what we wanted, and how to light it. I stopped her and told her I wasn't going to tell her a thing. She was the expert, and I trusted her opinion, so she should do whatever she felt was best. She was shocked by that, since she was so used to being told what to do. That went back to me believing in the people who worked for me. She did a much better job than I would have done, so I just let her go nuts.

I thought it was a cute little show, but a lot of guests didn't. Kitchen Kabaret was a beloved attraction to them, so they didn't want it to be replaced. But, I think eventually Food Rocks won people over, even though it was only there for 10 years. Part of the stage is still there, though, just behind the walls of the queue for Soarin'.

Overall, The Land was a pretty huge undertaking. It was 5 acres, all under one roof, and it was the largest pavilion in all of EPCOT. It had the highest capacity and the highest attendance of any of the other pavilions for the first few years. I was always really proud of that.

I also did the design for the Electric Umbrella restaurant, too. It was originally called Stargate Restaurant, but that entire area was going through a re-design in the mid-1990s. The name came about one day in a meeting, when some guy asked if we would be interested in electric umbrellas to sell in EPCOT. They literally were electric umbrellas, because they had some lights on the top of them. Well, the design of them stunk, but I absolutely loved the name, and thought it would be a great title for the new restaurant. In fact, when we pitched the idea to Michael Eisner, he liked the name so much that he wanted to name the whole damn building the Electric Umbrella! Obviously, that idea got squashed, and it turned out to be called Innoventions.

There was a bank on Wilshire Boulevard in Beverly Hills years ago that had the rear fender of a Chevy on the wall. It had the steering wheel and a tire, and the whole thing had these neon tubes running all around it. I thought it was a beautiful piece of pop art. When it came time to do the mural in The Electric Umbrella, I remembered that piece, and wanted to do something like it. I made it with all those neon lights, and added fake rain coming down, and I just thought it looked neat.

My obsession with propellers made its way into EPCOT eventually, too. When they were changing CommuniCore into Innoventions, I thought the entire centerpiece of the plaza was dead. In fact, that was always one of my biggest complaints about EPCOT. You walked through the turnstile, and nothing was moving. Unlike Disneyland, where they have pieces moving around all over the place.

Electric Umbrella, as seen today at EPCOT.

EPCOT, to me, portrayed a very static future, so I suggested we add some of my propellers in there. I talked them into building them like lampposts throughout the whole Park. When I was talking to Bob Gurr about it, he told me to make them electric. He said I couldn't trust the wind to work in Florida all the time. So we made them electric so they would always be in motion. The other thing I did was something I'd always loved seeing on hot rods. You know how a lot of hot rods have that paint with the glitter built right into it? Well, I had the columns sprayed just like that, to give them a little more life. If I had known about that stuff back when I built the Tower of the Four Winds, I would have had them do the same to that as well.

As we were working on all this, we realized there really wasn't much there for young kids to do. Scott Hennesy came up with the idea for a pavilion called EPTOT, which would have been for little kids. We made a model of our idea to show to Management. Each section of the model represented a little kid version of all the pavilions located in EPCOT. There was one for The Living Seas, one for The Land, and so on. It was basically a mini play area based on all the big pavilions. We thought it would be a great little addition, but Marty Sklar and John Hench shot us down. They thought EPCOT was strictly for adults, and not for children. Years later, when Eisner took over, he heard about EPTOT, and thought it was a great idea. He changed the name to Kidcot, and we were going to design some of that as well. My involvement with that died also and Kidcot turned into something completely different.

As you can tell, my work for EPCOT is an incredible story all of its own, because there are so many different parts to it. The amount of hours I spent working on various things there was unbelievable. I was lucky, though, because I really believe I had the best team there. The group of people that I worked with were just absolutely incredible and, even if some of the things we designed never got built, I still feel like we did a marvelous job.

Before we move on, I'd really like to talk about John Hench for a minute. From this chapter, it may seem that we didn't like each other, but we actually did. You have to remember that John trained me. He was my mentor. When I first started at WED, I didn't know what I was doing half the time. Whenever they gave me an assignment, I would go into John's office after work, and he'd sit there for a few hours with me going through everything. He really helped me out a lot, and he was a real sweetheart for doing that.

He was a marvelous teacher as well. It was a shame, though, because no one would ask for his help because they thought it would make them look weak. That wasn't true, though. I mean, how else are you supposed to learn? I think John respected that I came to him, and I respected him for kind of taking me under his wing. I thought he did a hell of a job teaching me.

The thing was, we just loved to fight with each other. I don't know what it was, but we just really went at it. There was never really any mean-spiritedness behind it. It was just something we did. Because he trained me, I understood his way of thinking and the way he worked.

John had a sneaky way of fighting with folks though. Whenever someone was arguing with him about a certain subject, he'd ask a question about something else to throw them off balance. When he would do that, people wouldn't know what to do. But when he did it with me, I'd say, "That's not what we're talking about, let's get back to that."

IT'S KIND OF A CUTE STORY

We had a lot of respect for each other, though. He would never say it in front of other people, but he admired me for standing up for what I believed in. The last time I went back to work at WED, I went up to see John, and we talked for a little bit.

"Now that you're back, maybe we can get things straightened out around here a little bit," he said to me. So, while we loved and respected each other, we just loved to do battle. No one would battle with him the way I did, so he really relished that. It was always a love and hate thing with us.

After I finished up my assignments for EPCOT, they started thinking about doing a refurbishment for Fantasyland in Disneyland. Because of how costly EPCOT was, Management didn't want to spend a significant amount of money on anything at Disneyland, though. That meant no new rides or attractions. That was completely out of the question. They just didn't have the budget.

There was a real talented little gal named Raellen Lescault who worked in the drafting department at Disney. She had grown up with Disneyland, and went there her entire childhood. When she was old enough, she got a job as one of the tour guides. Eventually, she wound up in drafting. When she heard that they weren't going to spend any money, she came up with a fantastic idea on how to update Fantasyland while spending very little money.

She showed me her ideas, and they looked great. It definitely wouldn't have cost them anywhere close to what a new attraction would have. She wanted to present her ideas to upper Management, so I set it up for her. I really believed in her ideas, so I thought Card Walker and Ron Miller, who were in charge at the time, would like them, too.

She gave them her little spiel, and they loved it. They put the number crunchers on it to figure out the cost, and it came back that it was right on the money. It was a go. I was happy for her because she was going to make the dreams she had a reality, and I was going to help her do it.

The next thing we know, Tony Baxter comes in, and decides he wanted to work with her on it. Work with her? He didn't work with her; he took it away from her and made it his own! This was just one example of how things were being handled by management, and in my opinion, it was very unprofessional. I realized at that point that my time at Disney was coming to an end again.

A mobile I designed still hangs from the ceiling of the old Wonders of Life pavilion,
even though you can only see it when the pavilion is open for special events.

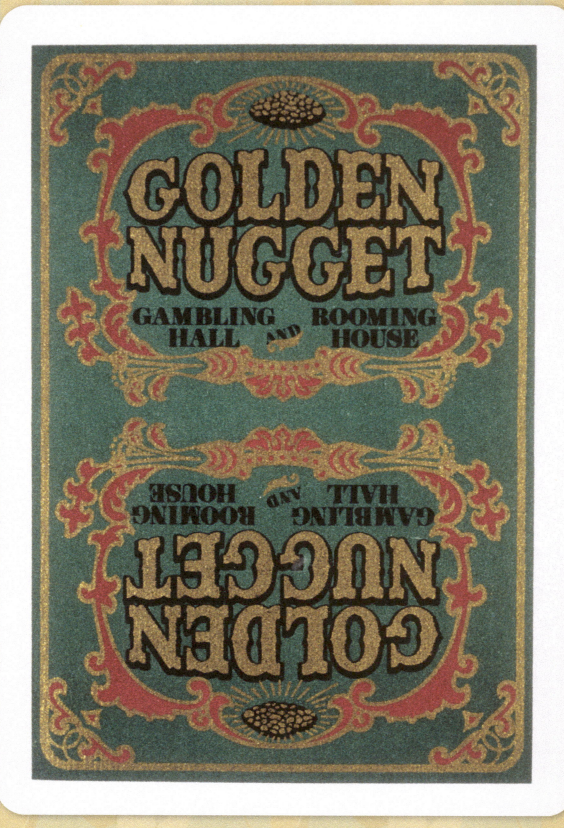

Playing card design I did for Steve Wynn.

CHAPTER 19

STEVE WYNN

lthough I was with Disney on and off for almost 40 years, I was also on the streets for 18 years as well. Not literally, of course, but figuratively. I didn't always have the financial support of working with Disney, but that was something I promised myself when I was very young; working for Disney was a dream come true, of course, but I also wanted to be able to stand on my own two feet, and support myself without being with a big company.

So, being on the streets was a very special experience for me because I didn't have that massive Company power behind me. I had to do things as they came. Honestly, after Walt passed, I actually preferred working on my own. The only problem was that there wasn't that much freelance work out there, while Disney remained a constant, steady stream of jobs. So, it was a rough decision.

One time when I was on my own, I read an article about this young guy in his early thirties, Steve Wynn, and how he just took over the Golden Nugget in Las Vegas. In the article, he stated that his idol was Walt Disney. I thought, 'Oh my God…this kid sounds like me.' So I wrote a little letter to Steve and said, "I used to work for Walt. If you'd ever like to meet with me, or have a project that I may be of assistance on, I'd love to talk with you."

Well, it was less than a week later that I got a call. Next thing I knew, I was on an airplane to fly out to Vegas to meet him. I got there, and we talked all day long. All he wanted me to do was tell him stories about Walt. It's so funny, because when I got up to leave, he turned to me and said, "I don't know how I could use you, Rolly, but I love hearing about Walt!"

Just before walking out the door, I looked down at the ugliest stationery I had ever seen. It was for the hotel, and it was just hideous! I turned to him and said, "Steve, let me re-design your stationery. If you like it, you can pay me. If you don't like it, you don't pay me."

"That's a deal, Rolly," he said.

I took a few days, and came back to him with a new design. Not only did he love it, but he told me he had some other things he'd like me to help him with. That's how I started consulting for him.

The first official job I did for him dealt with his first hotel that he built over at the Golden Nugget in Las Vegas. He didn't want

New stationery that I designed for Steve Wynn.

to go the traditional route, and just have an eighth floor or a twelfth floor. Instead, he wanted to name all of them after ghost towns. He wanted paintings of what the original ghost towns looked like on all the floors. I subcontracted some of my old painter friends from WED to do them. They each had their own floor and would do their own research for it. It was coming along nicely. I embossed the elevators with big brass doors that I did the design for. It looked really good.

I worked on and off with him for a while, and eventually went back to Disney. After working on EP-COT, and getting upset with WED again, I called Steve. He said, "Rolly, just get on a plane!" So, I got on a plane and made a deal to start working for him full-time.

The first thing he did was fly me to Atlantic City to take a look at this bird cage he had. It was this 50 foot bird cage in the lobby of his casino. He told me that the macaws they had in there flew up to the top, and just sat up there and pooped. He wanted me to take a look at it, and see if I could make some kind

of bird show out of it. He was looking for his own version of the Enchanted Tiki Room, pretty much, and I was happy to oblige. I got a hold of a couple of colleagues I liked from Disney, and away we went! I designed and developed this brand new bird show from scratch, using animatronic birds again.

An interesting bit about this story was that there were no moving eyes in the birds, just regular little eyes. Steve came to check it out one day, and we ran it for him a couple of times. Granted, we still had a long way to go on it, but he wanted to check out its progress. So he watched it and said he wanted moving eyes in the birds.

"I want the eyes to do this, I want the eyes to do that, and I want the eyes to do this and this, and I want eyelids!" He was very intent on eyes moving. So, Alvaro Villa, who was working on the show with me, turns to him and says, "Oh God Steve, that'll cost!" But Steve said he didn't care. That's what he wanted, and that's what he got.

Enchanted Tiki Room aside, I think we built the best damn bird show that was ever built. My understanding was

This page and opposite: Part of the bird show that was originally in Atlantic City, New Jersey.

IT'S KIND OF A CUTE STORY

that when he sold the Golden Nugget in Atlantic City, he took the bird show with him. He's got a casino in Laughlin, and I think the bird show is out there now, still up and running. I do know that he loved that show and I was very proud of it.

Steve and I stayed real close even when I kept bouncing around jobs. We always got along great. He would always call me by my full name, Roland Fargo Crump, whenever I'd see him. When I went back to WED for a while, I took him, his wife, and his girls on their own personalized tour of Disneyland whenever they came out. I learned a lot from Steve, and I also think he learned a lot from me.

One of the neatest things he did was when he called all of his employees in at the Atlantic City location one day. He got all 600 employees together and told them that he knew that things had been kind of tough lately. As compensation for all their hard work, he gave them all brand new cars. Can you believe that? He gave away 600 brand new Chevys! I thought to myself, 'Here is a man that gives. He knows how to be a businessman, but he also knows how to treat his employees.' I thought that was incredible.

The fact that Steve loved Walt so much carried over into his work, and he tried to do everything the way Walt would have. To find someone like that, especially another head executive, was just wonderful and refreshing for me because I loved working with Walt so much. In fact, I told Steve that one day. I told him that he was the only person I've ever met that's another Walt Disney. Oh God, he loved that. He'd always say, "Would you bring that up at dinner tonight with these guests that I'm having over?"

It was really true though because Steve was a stickler for detail. Everything had to be immaculate, and he took care of everyone.

Enjoying my time onboard *Calypso*.

CHAPTER 20

THE COUSTEAU SOCIETY

round 1983, I got a phone call from Jean-Michel Cousteau, who is the son of famed ocean explorer Jacques Cousteau. Jean-Michel said that he was coming to Las Vegas and wanted to have dinner with me. I thought that was kind of neat, to have dinner with a Cousteau, so of course I agreed. I had met Jean-Michel before, but it was a long time before that call. Back when California brought the *Queen Mary* over to Long Beach, they asked The Cousteau Society to put an exhibit in her to explain what they were all about. I remember going to see it, and meeting him there, very briefly. Honestly, it was a piece of crap, because they didn't know what they were doing. But, it was very popular because their name was associated with it.

Anyway, I went to meet Jean-Michel for dinner. I was pretty busy before that, working on all the projects for Steve Wynn, and Jean-Michel told me what a hard time he had getting in touch with me, but he was glad he finally did. He told me he had been to Disneyland recently, and fell madly in love with all the illusions in the Haunted Mansion. He loved it so much that he wanted someone to design something similar for him. He knew I was associated with the Mansion way back when, so he wanted to hire me to do it! He knew I didn't do much with the current attraction, but he enjoyed my work and wanted me to use some illusions, much like in the Haunted Mansion, for an Ocean Center Pavilion.

I was flattered, so of course I agreed. It was pretty good timing, too, because Wynn didn't have any more work for me and I was getting ready to leave. The next hotel that he was going to build was canceled, so I was just sitting there like a bump on a log. So I figured why not go and work for the Cousteaus for a little while?

We decided on a pretty good fee for my services, so I was happy. I came back to California, and started working out of the Cousteau office on Santa Monica Boulevard. I started doing my homework on it immediately, and I basically read everything I possibly could about them to try to get to know them better. I went through all their files and watched all their films, just to get a good grasp on them.

I loved Jacques Cousteau from the second I met him. He was a riot, and had a great sense of humor. The first time he saw me, he said, "I always hated Walt Disney and I also hated Mickey Mouse." All I said was, "Oh okay," and shook his hand. But then he started cracking up. He was just messing with me. He was a great guy like that.

One time, I had lunch with him and about 30 other people on top of this beautiful building in Monaco. It was a wonderful lunch, but the problem was they all spoke French. Of course, I don't speak a word of it, so I had no idea what was going on. So I just sat there during the meal, eating, and not really interacting with anyone. When it was over, I pulled Jacques aside and asked what the deal was. He looked at me, and kind of winked with this sly smile.

"You know," he said, "This lunch was in your honor. It's just a shame they all spoke French!" With that, he started to laugh. Such a great sense of humor he had.

One of the first things they did after that was to invite me on *Calypso*, their famous research vessel, for a week. They wanted me to really get to know the people who worked for them, and see them in action. So, I went with them to the Amazon, near a little town called Iquitos. I got to spend some time with the divers, go into the decompression chamber and best of all, sleep on the deck! The boat was pretty full so they had to give me a makeshift bed but I didn't mind. It really was a once in a lifetime experience.

One of the best stories from that project was when I was on the boat and the Minister of the Interior (who was also the Minister of Tourism) came for a visit. He and Jacques were good friends, so he was just coming to say hello. There was a heliport of sorts on the back of *Calypso*, so the Minister flew in by helicopter.

Once he was all settled in, Jacques asked him if he wanted to go for a ride on the hovercraft. In case you don't know, a hovercraft was this fancy vehicle with big propellers that could travel on land and water. It was a pretty neat machine. Anyway, the Minister agreed.

My bed onboard *Calypso*.

Going along with him was another guest on the boat, Tim, along with this guy Falco, who was the best driver Jacques had. There was only enough room for the three of them, so Jacques said I could take the next ride out. I didn't mind so much, and I waved them off as they rode off up the Amazon.

A few hours pass, and I start to wonder about them. I found Jacques to see if he thought they were gone for quite a while. He assured me that they weren't, and that everything was fine. So I waited another few hours, and then it started to get dark.

Now Jacques started to panic a little bit. He came right out and said, "We've lost the Minister of the Interior."

Everybody just looked at him and said, "What the hell do you mean?!" But he meant exactly what he said.

"We lost him. We don't know where he is. We can't find the hovercraft!" Now I'm worrying even more, thinking the worst, and thanking God that I didn't get on that hovercraft!

Finally, they came back, but in a very odd way.

What happened was they were flying across the water when Falco took them up on land. As soon as they got on dry land, the hovercraft just stopped. The Minister of the Interior got a little concerned, but Falco assured him there was nothing to it. He said he was just going to hit the carburetor with a wrench, and it would be fine. So he started pounding on the carburetor for about a half hour, and it still wouldn't start.

Falco assured him again not to worry, that he'd contact *Calypso*. He got out his two-way radio, only to find that the batteries were dead. But again, Falco told them it would be okay, because *Calypso* would come find them if they didn't return after a few hours. By now, the sun was setting, and the mosquitoes were coming out. They were starting to bite the 3 of them, but Falco took out a can of that Off! insect spray and said not to worry. Just as he was about to spray it on the Minister, he realized that the can was empty! Luckily, there were a bunch of canvases on the hovercraft, so they covered themselves in them so they didn't get eaten alive.

The infamous hovercraft that wound up being stranded in the Amazon.

A few years before that, the government gave out these little dugout canoes made from trees to people in the area. They had little motors on the back to help them get around faster. As the 3 guys are sitting there waiting, this guy in one of those canoes comes putting along the Amazon. The Minister of the Interior stands up, and yells to the guy, asking him to come over to them. He said he was the Minister of the Interior, and he was in need of a ride back to the ship.

The guy in the canoe said, "I don't care who you are; if you get me a can of gasoline and some Coca-Cola, I'll take you wherever you want to go!" The canoe was pretty small, so only the Minister came back in it. Once Jacques figured out where Falco and Tim were, he set off to get them. It was kind of funny, because when the Minister got back on the boat, Jacques asked him if he wanted a drink, and the Minister asked for a glass of vodka, straight up!

I left the boat not too long after that. When I was heading out, Jacques said to me, "Well, Rolly, what do you think of our Society?"

"You guys are nuts!" I said. "I see you on TV all the time, and everything is just fine, but that's a bunch of crap. You guys edit all of that crazy stuff out! I watched what happened the other day with the Minister of the Interior, and you guys fucked up big time!"

Cousteau was in hysterics over that. He had such a great sense of humor. He said, "You know, you're absolutely right about that!"

Anyway, when I got back, I started developing this Ocean Center for them. ABC called me to ask me if I was available to do some work. They wanted to get into the theme park business, and open some all over the world. I told them I was interested, but I was working with Cousteau at the moment and didn't have the time. They surprised me and said that was great, because that was probably going to be one of their first projects! Little did I know that ABC and The Cousteau Society had worked out a deal.

My business card for Mariposa Group.

Scale model of the Ocean Center for Norfolk, Virginia.

Of course, that made the Cousteaus happy because that meant they didn't have to pay me themselves. I would be working on someone else's salary, which was good because they really didn't have that much money to begin with. I was going to be working directly for them, but they wanted to subcontract me out. So, I formed Mariposa Design Group, and got a whole bunch of kids who I worked with at Disney to come work for me there, including my son.

The Cousteaus had plans to do a few Ocean Centers all over the world. One was going to be in New Jersey, because they had offices in Secaucus. I don't remember where exactly, but I know it was going be on some pier. Somebody told me that when they were visiting the site to survey it, it was a big abandoned warehouse. When they walked in, they found some guy hanging from the rafters in there!

All the guy selling the property could say was, "Well, this is New Jersey, you know how it is."

Another one was going to be in Norfolk, Virginia. The folks in Norfolk told The Cousteau Society that they could bring *Calypso* into their port when it was not out at sea. The city offered to pay for all the maintenance on it when it was needed, and in exchange, they wanted them to build their first Ocean Center there. Now all of a sudden, I was flying back and forth between Norfolk and California, working with the city planners and my designers.

I developed and designed a complete Ocean Center for them, which was very much like one of the pavilions you'd find at EPCOT. Jacques Cousteau was very happy with it, and we were getting ready to build it. Then, for financial reasons, they told me they were going to have to put it on hold for a little over a year. I was a little disappointed, but I understood. Besides, with Mariposa, we were working on a few different projects at once, so I just concentrated on those.

They came back to me about six months later, and told me they were ready to do the Ocean Center. Unfortunately, I was REALLY busy then. I just didn't have the time! I had about 6 different projects that I was doing at that time. But the point was, I didn't have the time for it, I didn't have the space, and I certainly didn't have the manpower.

They didn't know what to do but they really wanted to get going. To try to make it work, I told them that if they got a team together, and brought them over to my offices in L.A., I would teach them everything they needed to know. I would take them through the master plan, and make sure they understood just how everything needed to go.

In the very little spare time I had, I started working with this French team. It turned out that they were the same people who did that horrible exhibit in the *Queen Mary* all those years earlier. I didn't realize Jean-Michel was still connected to all those ding-a-lings! They were really nice but they didn't have a clue what they were doing. Meanwhile, they started flying me back and forth to Paris to work with the crew over there. I did my best, but I wasn't overseeing the entire project, just guiding them along, so there was only so much I could do. All of a sudden, the Art Director started changing everything. He wasn't listening to anything I said, and started changing the designs I had done. It got to be real messy. To make it even worse, Jean-Michel started messing with my designs, too.

As part of the Ocean Center, I designed a ride that took you to the bottom of the ocean in the middle of a storm. It was going to be a dark ride, and use a system very similar to

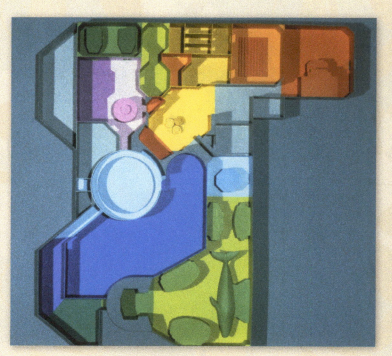

Overhead layout of the Ocean Center.

Scale model of the Omnimover ride that we designed to help teach guests about sea life.

the Omnimovers that Disney uses now. You would sit in this little pod for about four minutes, and take a trip to the bottom of the sea. It had some really interesting effects in there that I was proud of.

The whole idea was that you went on the ride, and then when you came out, you'd be on the bottom of the ocean. You could walk around down there, and check out all the exhibits. There were all these little theaters along the way that you could go into and learn about all about the Cousteaus and their research. There were a lot of hands-on exhibits in there.

Jean-Michel wanted some kind of exhibit in there that talked about the fish population. If you took all the fish in the ocean, and divided them up amongst everyone on the planet, everyone would get one million square inches of food. That's how much more sea life is in the ocean compared to people living on this planet! He wanted me to present facts like that some way, so I created a character called the God of the Sea. He was going to be an animatronic figure, and have this neat set with seaweed hanging around it. The seaweed would separate, and he would come out and introduce himself. Of course, the voice you heard was the sound of the ocean coming from the shell that made up his head!

In fact, his entire body was made out of different things that you would find in the ocean: fish, seaweed, coral, and pretty much everything. It would all come together to form this God of the Sea. I thought that would have been a neat touch. He was going to go into this great dissertation about the food in the ocean, and how valuable it is to the world. I just thought it was an interesting way to present that.

We also had a 90 foot blue whale that you could walk inside of. For some reason, Jean-Michel decided that he wanted everyone to see the whale first, and then go on the ride. And for that to happen, they would have to go on the ride backwards…it would start at the bottom of the ocean, and then go to the surface.

I told him that he wasn't following the storyline. The whole point was to take the ride to the bottom of the ocean, and that's how you got to explore the world down there. But he insisted we do it his way. I don't know what the hell he was thinking. It was just another one of those things that just fell apart because of it. All things considered, they did a fairly good job of it, despite all the changes. Some of the effects didn't work as well, since the whole attraction was now backwards, but they did the best they could with it. It would have been far better if they had left it the way it was, but it wasn't up to me.

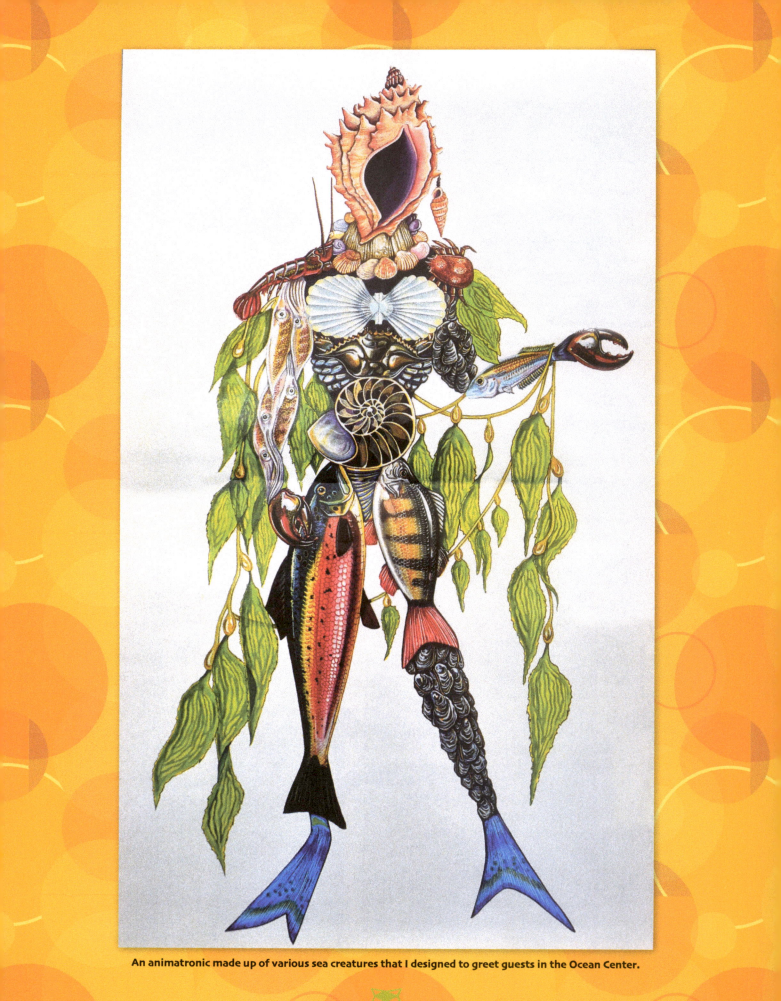

An animatronic made up of various sea creatures that I designed to greet guests in the Ocean Center.

IT'S KIND OF A CUTE STORY

Me showing Jacques Cousteau (middle) and Kristoff Renée, the architect (left), how I envisioned the Ocean Center.

It turned out that way for the rest of the project, too. They just stopped listening altogether, and then I didn't have the time to deal with it anymore. So, I left and went back to work on the other stuff I was doing with Mariposa.

Two weeks before they were about to open up, they invited me over to see what I thought of it. Much like I expected, it turned out to be a piece of crap. The French designers just ruined it, because they didn't do anything I'd told them to. I was pretty upset about that.

After going through the whole thing, I started looking for Jean-Michel, who was unsurprisingly nowhere to be found. So I told the Vice President of The Cousteau Society that I wouldn't work for them ever again because they didn't listen to me at all. They needed a project manager, and they just had a guy who didn't know what he was doing in charge. To make it worse, they had gone over budget. WAY over budget. Jacques Cousteau probably put in about a million of his own money, but they were still close to 10 million in the hole. It was just a mess. All of this was because Jean-Michel had this huge ego, and he wanted everything done his way. He didn't bring in the people that he should have, and didn't listen to reason.

They opened up anyway. To pay off their massive debt, they had to charge more than the public would accept. Hardly anyone went because it just wasn't worth the money. It was barely open 6 months before they started running into some serious problems. They eventually sold it to some Arab businessmen, who did the best they could with it but, 6 months later, the whole thing just went under.

During this time, Jacques Cousteau passed away, thank God. I mean, it's sad that he passed, because he was a great man, but he didn't live to see this project go under, which I thought was for the best. It would have just broken his heart.

It was kind of sad because I thought it was going to be a beautiful project. I remember telling Jacques, when I first started working on the Ocean Center, that I had enough information to build an entire educational theme park! Between the history of what the organization was and all the research they had done, I could have expanded it into this amazing thing. It wouldn't have been a big theme park, but it could have been about 20 acres. So, considering how it all went down, it always made me sad.

The outside of Fort Al Jalali.

CHAPTER 21

OMAN

There were a lot of people who left Disney to form their own companies, and did very well for themselves. There was a whole fraternity of us out there that worked together on outside projects, and we trusted each other. It was a family. There was this one company called Management Resources who were always finding jobs for me. They'd go into businesses that wanted to spark up their lobby or break-room or something.

Management Resources called me one day, back in 1984, and said, "Well, we got a job with a Dr. Zawawi." Dr. Zawawi was a man from Oman that had made a lot of money and really loved Disney. It's a really interesting story about how he made his small fortune.

When the current Sultan was a young man, his father (who was Sultan at the time) sent him to England. He put him in the Army there and said, "You learn how it's done, and then come back to Oman to build me an Army."

They never had an Army before, because they never needed one. But the old man wanted one anyway. Well, as the young son spent some time in England, he found out what the rest of the world was like. In Oman at that time, there were no radios, no TVs, no paved highways, and no public schools…it was about as far backwards as you could get.

So, when the kid saw all of this, he realized that he had to go back and change Oman but also build this Army that his father wanted. So he sat down with his Dad and said to him, "Hey, we've got to do this, we've got to do that, we've got to do this…we're like 50 years behind the times of the outside world!" The Sultan got mad at him. Very mad, actually. He didn't want to do any of those things! He just wanted his son to come back and build him an Army.

The son wouldn't let any of this stuff go, so the Sultan wound up putting him under house arrest. He became a prisoner in his own home. His father had guards all over the house so he couldn't get out. Well, Dr. Zawawi was a personal friend of his. The two of them had gone to school together. They were very, very close growing up, and he trusted him with his life. So, some way or another, he got to Zawawi and said, "You gotta get me out of here."

Somehow, Zawawi helped him escape his prison. He helped him put together a team of people that eventually turned into a rebellion. They took over the government! They didn't kill anyone, I don't think, but they took his father and sent him to England. They put him in a private home in England somewhere and the young Sultan took over. He started rebuilding Oman.

Based on his experiences outside the country, the first thing he did was to modernize the country. He put in streets, schools, hospitals, the whole nine yards. Despite being behind the times, they were a wealthy country, so they had the funds to do it pretty quickly. As a gift for helping him out so much, the young Sultan gave Zawawi a whole bunch of oil wells. He pretty much became a billionaire at that point. He bought his own 747 that he flew back and forth to the United States in.

Anyway, Management Resources said to me, "We have to go meet Zawawi and we want you to come with us."

There was a Portuguese fort built in Oman back around 1400 called Al Jalali. Before the young Sultan took over, it had been turned into a prison. It was pretty bad there…pretty much their equivalent of

The room at the top of Fort Al Jalali before we made it into a show teaching the history of Oman.

Guantanamo Bay. In fact, if you used the words "Al Jalali" over there, everybody would shake because that's where they did nasty things to people that went to prison.

Zawawi's idea was to completely refurbish the fort into something nice. He wanted to give the Sultan a place where he could invite the heads of state from all the other countries to come and learn about the history of Oman. He also wanted it to be a celebration of his country's greatness, and really show people that they weren't just this small, outdated little place. He planned on having armed guards standing at attention at its entrance to create an air of magnitude. He wanted to show it only to Kings, Queens, Presidents, and so on; folks in leadership positions.

Management Resources first hooked up with Zawawi because he met them when he was trying to buy a hotel at Walt Disney World. Obviously, Disney wouldn't sell one to him, and he was very upset about that! So instead, he decided on this renovation of Fort Jalali.

We got over there and they said, "Rolly, you've got to come up with an idea that allows people to learn about the history of Oman in 9 minutes."

Now, that was a pretty good little challenge. We toured the room he wanted it in, and I was a little worried. It was on the top floor of a tower of the fort, which was built in 1660, so it didn't seem like the most stable of places. It was just hotter than hell over there to begin with, too, so I thought the heat might have some effect on the longevity of the whole thing. But I thought to myself, if Kings and Queens are going to come in here, then damn it, I was going to give them a show to remember!

On the way back to where we were staying, I started visualizing what I was going to do. It actually came from an idea that I'd had in the back of my head for a long time. Every time Disney did something, there was an animatronic figure that spoke to you. You always knew where the voice was coming from because you had the point of reference of the figure. I always thought it would be great to do a show where there was no lip-sync, where this big booming voice just sort of spoke to you. So, I decided to have the room itself talk to you.

I got to work designing the whole interior right away. It really didn't take long once I got the ball

IT'S KIND OF A CUTE STORY

Another view of the room before we put the show in.

rolling. I had these big, empty trunks from Oman sent to me, and we put these amazing special effects in them. One of the parts of the show would talk about the 'jewels of the country.' All of a sudden, the trunk would open up, and there would be jewels sparkling inside, which were really fiber optics. They would talk about how the jewels were not diamonds or pearls, but the people of Oman, the culture itself. It was a beautiful effect, and just a beautiful little metaphor.

The next vignette had a little ship rocking back and forth, making it look like it was in the water. I had a shower door there with a special effect under it to simulate it being on the waves. You could hear the seagulls and the waves crashing in the background. The next area had all these khanjars and daggers, and you could hear the birds from out in the desert. The whole show had all these simple visual and audio cues like that in it that just really sold the illusion.

The neat thing about it was that it was all computerized, so it was done in every language. No matter who came in to see it, the show could run no matter what! If a Chinese delegate would come in, they'd just hit play on the Chinese voice-over track. It was amazing.

When we were finished, the Sultan had to approve it. We didn't get to meet him personally, but we heard that he'd watched the show and loved it. He began to call it his "talking room." He enjoyed it so much that he had the entire floor marbleized and weatherproofed so it would last a long time.

There is a cute little story about a dinner I had there one night. You see, Zawawi had this house specifically for dinner parties. He used to have these massive get-togethers with about 50 people at once, so he had to have somewhere to put them all. While we were working on the show, he always invited one of us to one of his famous parties. Each of us got a turn going, and he just treated us really, really well. We would sit right next to him, and he would make the servants wait on us hand and foot.

When it was my night to be his guest, I just had a blast. Just before dinner started, Zawawi told his guests that I did magic. He'd seen me doing some card tricks for one of the chefs the night before, and was pretty impressed. He told everyone at the table about it, and said if I was really treated right, I would give a magic show after dinner. He basically offered me up to the lions there, but we'll get to that later.

Anyway, dinner started. As we're eating, Zawawi leans over to me and asks how I'm enjoying my meal so far. I was on the second course of a 6 course meal, and I said it was just great. The night before, I had eaten dinner at the Colonel's house. The Colonel was a retired US military man who became Zawawi's right hand man. I had spicy chicken curry there, which Zawawi knew.

"How did you like it last night?" he asked me.

"I enjoyed it very much," I told him.

"Would you like some more of it?" he asked.

"Well, sure, I suppose so," I replied.

He snapped his fingers in the air, and said loudly "Bring on the spicy chicken curry!"

One of the waiters came over, and whispered in Zawawi's ear that they didn't have any spicy chicken curry. He turned to me and told me so, and I said that was fine.

"No, no, don't worry," he said. "They'll have it in just a few minutes." Apparently, when you asked him for something, he had to deliver it. And he did! A few minutes later, I had it in front of me. I started eating it when he turned to me again.

"How are you enjoying it?"

The finished product.

"It's fine. It could be a little spicier, though," I said off handedly, not really thinking anything of it. But Zawawi's hand shot up and snapped again.

"Bring on some SPICIER chicken curry!" he said. The waiters scrambled, and a few minutes later, I had another bowl in front of me, with even spicier chicken curry in it. I was kind of embarrassed by that, but I started to eat it so I wouldn't offend him. It was super spicy this time, though, and my face was getting a little red.

"Would you like something to drink?" Zawawi asked me.

"Oh, sure. How about a Miller Lite?" I asked. His hand shot up again as he snapped his fingers.

"Bring on the Miller Lite!" he said. Well, none of the guys there had even heard of Miller Lite before! Zawawi apologized profusely, but I told him it was really fine, I'll just take any old beer they had. They wound up giving me a Heineken instead.

I was amazed at how the waiters and servants were responding to his every beck and call, though. I told one of them that the last time I saw someone like him, he had green skin and was much larger, like a genie coming out of a magic lamp! All he had to do was snap his fingers, and boom, it was there!

He laughed, and we started kidding with each other back and forth. Everybody was amazed to see how relaxed he was, and how much he was joking with me. He never did that with anyone else…mostly because nobody else did it with him! We just had a wonderful time.

Then the drinks started to flow more and more. We were getting pretty drunk by the time dessert came around.

"What would you like for dessert? Zawawi asked me.

"How about some apple pie?" I said. Again, his hand shot up and he snapped.

"Bring on the apple pie!" Of course, the waiter came over again and said they didn't have any. Zawawi told me to wait a little bit, and they would make one. They found a can of apple sauce in the back, and they made a quick pie out of that, and 15 minutes later, we had apple pie.

After dessert, I was pretty full, and pretty loaded. Zawawi announced that it was time to head down to the beach. It was 2 in the morning, and I was ready for bed. But not wanting to insult him, we all headed down to the beach.

They had this huge bonfire going down there, with a bunch of pillows and blankets set up around it for us to sit on. Most of us walked…or staggered…down there. Once I plopped down, 2 decks of cards were put in front of me. It was time for my magic show, apparently!

As far as I was concerned, I put on a good magic show. Granted, I was pretty drunk, so my memory of it may have been a little hazy, but I thought it went well. However, Zawawi's son was there, and he told me later that the next time I came over, he'd be sure to bring a real magician. I got a kick out of that.

The next day, I was nursing a little hangover while we were working when Zawawi showed up. Now, he didn't just show up by himself…he brought his entire harem of girls with him. He had about 5 beautiful women on his arms.

"I just wanted to let you know that the ladies here really enjoyed your magic show last night," he told me. Then he winked at me and smiled before walking out. It was too funny.

It was probably around 1985 when we finished the project. I honestly didn't think it would last more than a few years. Funny enough, though, I was doing some consulting work with a firm in 2007 who were designing a theme park for Dubai. I met a woman from Dubai who was kind of another consultant on the project. She was a younger gal, in her twenties or so. We were chatting one day, and I said to her, "You know, I did a show for Al Jalali once." She looked at me and said, "Wait a minute, I saw that show not too long ago!"

I looked at her kind of amazed, and was kind of like "…what?!" She described the entire show to me, in detail. I was amazed that it was still up and running…and continues to run to this day! Here I was, thinking it wouldn't last more than a year, and it's still going strong almost 30 years later. When I was over there, I didn't know if they would have any people that could run and maintain the computers for that long. I'm thrilled that show is still going. I'm very proud of that show.

CHAPTER 22

Design 27

Aside from all the stuff I talked about so far, I did a lot of work on various other projects throughout my life with my design firms. Some I just had a small hand in, while others I was with from start to finish. You see, when I left Disney, my name started to get passed around to other companies. They heard that I quit, so they started contacting me to do some work for them.

Within a year, I was working for all sorts of outside companies. I was making enough money that I was able to hire employees, which was great. As other folks I enjoyed working with left Disney, I asked them to come work for me. It was just great. We did a lot of fantastic projects.

One of the things that is probably most recognizable, but is never traced back to me, is the logo for Ernie Ball Guitar Strings. If you're a musician, you probably know what they are. Ernie was a kid I went to high school with that I was sort of friendly with. We didn't keep in touch after that, but we reconnected one day when I was in a park with my daughter. I was pushing her on a swing, and the guy standing next to me pushing his son looked really familiar. I couldn't quite place it until he said "Roland, is that you?"

Back then, he wasn't Ernie Ball. He was actually Roland Sherwood Ball. He changed his name to Ernie because he thought it sounded better. We got to talking about what we were up to those days. I told him I was working at Disney in Animation, and he said he was giving guitar lessons out of his house. He was also a studio musician on some Western TV show, but that didn't pay all that well, so most of his money came from guitar lessons.

We kept in touch after that, and one day he asked me to design his business card. I did it for him for $3, and he just loved it. He wanted to hire me to do some more design work for him, since he was getting into the business of selling guitar strings. So, I started to design all of his logos, his product's packages and even his Christmas cards! From then on, every design I did I got $5 for. Ernie was providing me with a whole bunch of extra cash, which is always nice to have. I did a whole bunch of freelance work for him for years.

Ernie was one of the reasons I started Design 27 to begin with. He always said I should have my own company, and he would hire me to work for him full-time. It wasn't until years later, after Walt passed and I left Disney, that I finally did just that. Of course, by then, I was doing work for a lot of other folks, so I couldn't work for him full-time.

There is another little story about my dealings with Ernie. Every once in a while, he'd come up to my office to hang out, and we'd just get ripped off of wine. On one of those nights, Ernie was looking at my walls, and saw the doper posters hanging on them. He was admiring them, and I told him about some of the other designs I came up with, including some for condoms.

I told him all about them, and he said what a great idea it would have been to actually make them. I thought about it for a moment and said, "Well, why the hell can't we do that?" I figured with Ernie's backing, we could go into the condom business together. We could come up with jokey designs for the boxes, similar to the doper

This page: **Design 27's logo.** • *Opposite:* **My team at Design 27 (I'm in the middle of the top row).**

posters, and we'd be set. We figured that Ernie could buy the rubber in bulk, and we'd package them in my boxes and sell them to local businesses. Back in those days, condoms weren't just out on display. You had to go up to the counter and ask for them. We thought that if the boxes didn't really advertise the fact that they contained condoms, but instead had some sort of crazy design on it, business owners would be more willing to leave them out.

The next day, I went out and bought some boxes of Trojans. I brought them back to the office to measure them, and then got to work doing my own box design. Within a few hours, I had a few of my own little condom boxes. I called them Capons, because that was another name for a rooster, and I had a picture of one on the cover. I chose to use a rooster for obvious reasons, but if you don't get it, think about some other names you call a rooster.

Ernie let me borrow one of his employees, and together we set out to look for a rubber manufacturer who would work for us. We contacted all of them, but unfortunately, none were interested.

Eventually, we had a meeting with Allied Latex, one of the largest rubber manufacturers in the world at the time. We presented it to them, and they loved the idea. They couldn't approve it right away, though, because they had to run it by their Board of Directors. In the meantime, they suggested we come up with other jokey names, because if these were a hit some other company was sure to come up with their own.

When I got back to the Design 27 offices, I mentioned this to the people working for me, and we came up with a whole list of different names and slogans. We just had a blast with them. We had Beavers ("Put a Beaver on your log"), Patriots ("Old Patriots never die, they just shrivel up"), and E Pubic Unum ("A '76 is better than a '69"). We made up mock-ups for all of these, just in case we needed them.

Finally, Allied got back to us and had to decline. The Board of Directors decided against it because every piece of rubber has a number stamped on to let you know who made it. If word got out that Allied was getting into the condom business, they would have a lot of problems with their advertisers and the public. It was a risk they didn't want to take.

It was a real shame, though, because I thought Capons would have been a hit, especially on college campuses. I wanted to do a whole line of bed sheets, pillow cases, t-shirts, the whole nine yards, with the Capon logo on it. I came up with a whole product line with other stuff, too, like the Zeus Jock Straps ("Guaranteed not to snag your bag," "Have a profile of the Gods," "Protect your family tree with the Olympian

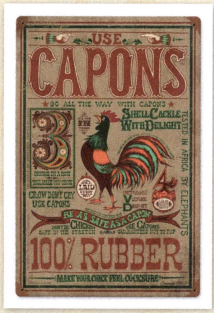

My original design for Capons, before they were made into mock-ups.

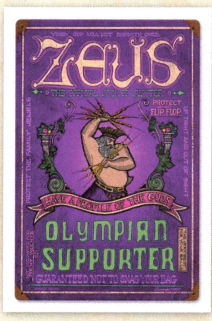

One of my other humorous posters, this time for Zeus Jock Straps.

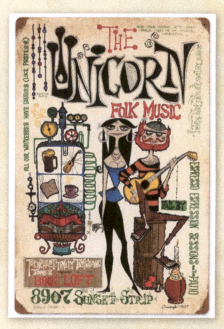

One of my posters from the 1960s, showing my offbeat sense of humor. This was one of many that were featured in the background of an episode of *The Dick Van Dyke Show*.

IT'S KIND OF A CUTE STORY

supporter"). We just had fun with it. I still think something like that would sell today!

As another note, aside from the doper and Capon posters, I also did some political satire ones in the early 1960s for poster pioneer Howard Morseburg's Esoteric Poster Company. They were satirizing communism, Cuba and the Soviet Union. I enjoyed making those posters, but they are noteworthy for another reason. I just recently found out that some of them were featured on *The Dick Van Dyke Show* in 1965. In the Season 4 episode, "Stacey Petrie Part 2," there are a few scenes where they are in a coffee shop. A lot of the artwork on the walls are my posters about Cuba. I thought that was pretty neat!

There was a fellow by the name of Chuck Corson who had been an assistant in the entertainment department at Disneyland. After he left, he called me and said he was putting together a show in Las Vegas.

Here I am, getting in there to make sure all the details are right.

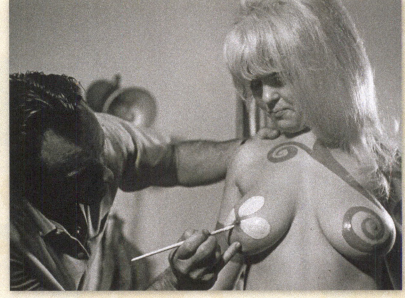
I'm very hands on with my work.

"I need your help," he said. "We're going to have a bunch of girls on stage, and we're going to project tattoos onto them. But I need to paint one of the girls up. Could you help me with that?" I didn't really have any idea what he meant by 'paint her up' but it was some extra cash, so who was I to say no?

He brought this beautiful girl over, who was a bar entertainer. The second we were all in the room together, the girl took off all her clothes. I was like, "Wait, what's going on?"

Chuck explained that he wanted me to do some designs with body paint on her. He told me the basic idea of what he wanted, and let me just go to town. It took me two and a half hours, and 2 six-packs of beer to paint her. It was fun, though, and we all had a great time. When they left, they put her in a raincoat so none of it would come off. I remember Chuck telling me later that she'd told him it took a lot of showers to get all of that paint off.

It was funny while we were doing it, though, because she said to me, "I don't know whether to run out of here or throw you on the floor and jump on top of you."

I gave her a wink and said, "Don't do that, you might smear the paint."

There is also a mall in Texas that I designed. I did this little fishing village in San Francisco once, which had this Victorian looking lighthouse as part of it. This developer saw it, and hired me right away to do this project he was calling Crossroads Mall.

He wanted to build this outdoor mall based on some he'd seen in Europe. Within 3 months, I designed the master plan of this whole shopping mall for him. I had a model built for him, and I even did a cost estimate so he'd have a good idea how much money he would spend on it. I designed it so that each section was inspired by a different country. One section looked straight out of Italy, another like it was right

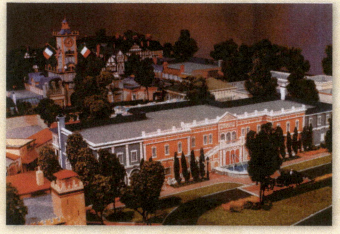

Scale model of Crossroads Mall, showing the "Italy" section in the front, with "France" in the back.

The "Italy" section of Crossroads Mall, as seen in its constructed form.

The "France" clock tower, as seen in its constructed form.

Close-up details of the scale model of the Crossroads Mall.

out of France. He loved it! He got the money right away, and they started to build it. I had to leave before they started, because I was about to go work on Circus World, but it was finished in no time. The guy loved it so much, though. It was a hit, too. He made a lot of money off of it. So much so that he went out and bought two Rolls-Royce automobiles. He even had custom license plates that said 'CROSSROADS' on them.

Unfortunately a few years later, the developer died of a heart attack. His wife and two sons didn't have the marketing sense he did, so within a year the place went bankrupt. They sold it off, and it became a school for a long time. These days, I hear that it was turned back into a mall.

There were a series of pushdowns I did as well, which were pretty cute. Some were just little novelty pieces and others were piggy banks. But I did a whole line of them, and the guy who manufactured them gave me $50 for every design I did. They continued doing them long after I stopped designing them, and to be honest, the new designs were kind of terrible.

The piggy banks I did didn't take off, because the manufacturers wanted to build them out of plastic since it was cheaper. I wanted them to be wood. I thought the wood would make them last longer, and just look nicer. I had one of a bakery truck with a bandit out front. You'd push his arm down, and a little sign would come up that said "Gimme the dough." When you did that, money would fall out of the back of the truck. Another one was of an angel, where you would push her down and a sign would pop up saying "Pennies From Heaven" as your money came out. Just some real cute stuff.

While we're on the subject of Design 27, we decided to have a little fun with the bathrooms we had in the office. Instead of having them a simple color, we painted them completely black. We hung pieces of chalk along the wall, and within a month, we had some of the best damn graffiti that you had ever seen. Irvin Feld, the guy from Circus World, came over to the office once, and had to use the bathroom. He came out

IT'S KIND OF A CUTE STORY

what seemed like an hour later and said we should have put a turnstile in there, and have people pay us to be entertained. We wanted to try to market something like that to bars, but the idea never took off.

This one time, we were designing a restaurant for a fellow, and we had to take the plans down to City Hall to get them approved. One of the gals in my office took them down to the planning department, and the woman behind the counter there was checking them over.

"These look almost like Disney drawings," she said.

"We all worked for Disney, so that's probably why," said the gal from my office.

"Oh, really? Well, did you know I designed the Tower of the Four Winds for the World's Fair?" said the woman at the planning department. The gal from my office stifled her laughter, let the woman finish, and then came back to the office to tell me.

As soon as I heard, I immediately said "I've got to call this woman and mess with her." I picked up the phone and gave her a call.

"My name is Roland Crump. I sent some drawing out to you earlier. I understand you designed the Tower of the Four Winds for the World's Fair?"

"Yes, I did," she replied.

"That's really funny," I said, "Because all these years, I thought that I designed it."

The phone went dead. I always laugh about that.

An assortment of pushdowns designed by me.

One of the many pushdown banks I designed.

Trying to fit in with the other dummies.

CHAPTER 23

OTHER THEME PARKS

Because of my obvious background in theme parks, I got a lot of job offers to consult on these. I only did the ones that I was interested in, though.

For example, there was a potential job in Magic Mountain, which is part of the Six Flags chain in California. They contacted me because they had a dark ride which they thought could use some work. It was already designed and built by a local guy, but they wanted me to take a look to see if I could do anything to improve it. I rode through it once and said "No thanks, not interested." All the damage was already done, and it just wasn't worth it for me to gut it and do it right. I always got a kick out of it when people who didn't understand the philosophy of a dark ride did one and then didn't understand why it wasn't meshing with the public. I may have been starving to death, but I still refused something that I didn't feel good about.

AstroWorld was a park in Houston, Texas. I wound up designing all their walkaround characters, and a new section of the park called Country Fair. It was a small area, but I did all the graphics, the exterior of the buildings, and a carousel. In fact, that was one of the first jobs I ever did with Design 27.

Some exterior design work for AstroWorld.
Opposite: Concept art for Marvel McFey, a walkaround character I designed for AstroWorld.

Concept art for Marvel McFey's cart I designed to go with the walkaround character.

The character and his cart, in their final form, entertaining at AstroWorld.

Kahe Point is one of those crazy stories that I love to tell. There were these two brothers from St. Louis who owned a meat packing company. They loved Hawaii, and they wanted to build a theme park there based on the history of the islands. They had tons of money, so they figured why not?

They flew me out there to check out the land and to do some research on Hawaii. It was a decent sized property they had, about 30 acres or so. When I came home, I did the master plan and had some of my employees do some illustrations for it. I sent all that off to them and they were ready to build.

We flew back out there again to present it to the government there, and they said

IT'S KIND OF A CUTE STORY

okay. But first, the brothers needed to get a building permit. And the only way to get one of those was to pay the government guys a quarter of a million dollars, under the table. It was a little fishy, but the brothers did it, and that was that. The government assured us the permit was on its way.

Now, Kahe Point is in a very rural part of Oahu. The people who lived there weren't too happy with what we were going to do. We were asked to give a presentation to them about the park to win them over. As each of us got up to say our piece, we were met with stony faces. Some of the locals sitting right behind us whispered into our ears that we had better leave after the presentation, otherwise they'd beat the crap out of us!

Luckily, the brothers hired this Samoan chief to be our bodyguard. He brought along a couple of his guys, and as long as we were with them, we were safe. But the locals just kept harassing us! One night, while we were there, this guy reeking of marijuana came running after us, screaming that they "…didn't want a goddamn theme park near our homes!" He was just going wild. There was one other guy that I was working with who was with me, and we both looked at each other and said "Let's get the hell out of here." We caught the next plane back home. We found out later that where they wanted to build the park is where the locals had their own little marijuana farm. If we built there, they would lose all of that, and they certainly didn't want to.

We told the brothers that we would gladly come back once they got the building permit. Unfortunately, they never did. The government guys kept asking for more money, and more money, and more money. Eventually, one of the brothers died of a heart attack and the other went broke. That was a shame because it really would have been a beautiful park.

Fabuland was a proposed theme park I did some consulting work on over in Paris, France. They invited me over for a week to listen to their ideas, and guide them along. They already had their own architect, their own designer, and their own ideas. I really have no idea what they wanted me for, but I went anyway. I sat there for one week, listening to them talk in French, with my interpreter trying her best to keep up. It was pretty clear that they had already decided what they wanted to do with their park, and even though their plan didn't make an ounce of sense to me, they were going to do it regardless of whatever I said.

I did some re-working of their master plans, and got my fee from them. After that, the whole thing just fell apart, like usual, because they couldn't get financing for it. I didn't mind, because I got a week in France!

There is one really good story about that week, though. The guy in charge would take us out to eat every night. They wouldn't go to dinner until ten o'clock over there, and dinner wouldn't even show up until close to midnight. A few days in, I was getting pretty sick of eating so late, let alone not being able to understand what was being said.

So my interpreter, who was a great little gal, said she would take me out to eat one night. She asked me where I wanted to go and I said, "I could really go for some Chinese food." We got in her car, and we went to this really strange part of Paris. She parks and says, "We're going to walk down these alleys now."

We're walking along, and she's saying to me, "We're looking for cats."

I did a double take at her.

"Looking for cats?!"

"Yes, because if we walk down an alley, and we don't see any cats, we don't go into any of those Chinese restaurants!" I was floored. Luckily, we didn't dine on cat that night. It was funny, because after dinner, she took me down to where the streetwalkers worked. All of them were down there, showing off their wares. There was this guy in a business suit, holding a briefcase, talking to one of them.

"What are they doing?" I asked.

"Oh, they're negotiating," she replied. Paris was a crazy place.

George Millay was the man who started SeaWorld. He was there for years, but he eventually got into trouble with his own Board of Directors, and they fired him. As soon as he left, he had this idea for a water park. He thought building that park would be a good way to get back at them. He hired me to help design it. I did the entire layout, along with the coloring and the logo. George was actually born on the 4th of July, so he had me color everything in red, white, and blue.

He told me once that SeaWorld made a lot of money when he was there, so in turn, he made a lot of money. He gave his wife a million dollars and said, "If anything ever happens to me, this is for you to put

The entrance to the ABC Wildlife Preserve.

away for a rainy day." After he got fired, he went to his wife and said, "Honey, remember that million dollars? I need to borrow it back for a bit to build this park." She refused! I thought that was too funny.

Eventually, he did get the financing and we were able to build the park. We were in a meeting one day, and he couldn't come up with a name for it.

"It's water, and it's wet. How hard can it be?" he kept saying. Eventually, I threw out the name Wet 'n Wild and he loved it. It stuck from there.

Some African-inspired folk art on the *World of the Wild* show building.

George was a character, though. Back when he was still with SeaWorld, he had 6 company cars that he borrowed. The only reason he had 6 was because he had no idea where any of them were! He would drive somewhere, get really drunk, and then take a cab home. But then he wouldn't remember where he parked the car, so they all just went missing. No wonder his wife wouldn't loan him that money back. Anyway, there are a bunch of Wet 'n Wilds all over the country now.

George, in a roundabout way, got me hired to do the ABC Wildlife Preserve. One of ABC's Vice Presidents was a good friend of George. They were looking for a designer for an animal park in Largo, Maryland that they were trying to get off the ground, and George recommended me. The park was already there before they came along, but they were trying to spruce it up.

IT'S KIND OF A CUTE STORY

They flew me out to interview and look at my portfolio before they hired me. Now, it's worth mentioning that, at the time, I was going through what I now call my 'crazy' period. I had a beard, rings all over my fingers, and I was wearing a Levi suit. I went out to New York to meet them looking like a hippie.

When I got there, I knocked on their door, and the guy who opened it just looked at me.

"I'm Rolly Crump," I told him.

"I was afraid you were going to say that," he replied.

But he let me in, and we got started. The President of ABC was there as well, and he didn't even bother looking at my portfolio. I brought 3 huge books with me to show them, and he just brushed them off.

"Oh no, we don't need to look at those. I'm a good friend of Donn Tatum's," he told me. Donn was the President of The Walt Disney Company at that time. This guy called Donn to ask about me and Donn said I was one of their best designers. That was all he needed to hear.

Basically, what I did for them was some drafting. I re-designed all the buildings, because they were just cement blocks with no theme. Since it was an animal park, I gave them all an African theme. The artwork was a little primitive, to fit with the theme. It all turned out kind of neat.

There is a funny story, about the music they played throughout the park. It was all contemporary jazz music. It blew my mind. I said, "You've got a park based on Africa, you don't want to hear jazz!" They didn't know what to do. I told them they were ABC, they had to have a vault full of sound effects of birds, monkeys, and lions that they could use. They claimed that they didn't, so I said I'd take care of it.

I went to Tower Records in L.A., and they had a section of nothing but sound effects. I bought a whole bunch of them, went through it with an audio guy, and created an entire soundtrack for the park. They were one of the biggest entertainment companies in the world, and they just couldn't figure out how to get animal sounds. It blew my mind, but I got it done.

The good news was that attendance for the park doubled the first year it was open. People really seemed to enjoy it. The bad news was that they didn't really know what they were getting into. The park was in Maryland, so during the winter months, they couldn't figure out why the animals weren't outside. They didn't factor in the snow either, and how that would affect attendance. Finally, they closed it down because they couldn't afford it anymore.

There was another project in Hawaii, on the North Shore of Oahu, at a place called the Kahuku Sugar Mill. It was an authentic Mill back in the day, but it was no longer open. There was a marketing guy who hired me to turn it into a museum of sorts. It was a historical place, so they wanted some attractions to teach people all about it.

I built them a theater inside the Mill. I made a preshow area that showed off some antiques from the Mill, along with some exhibits at the end. I also designed costumes for the people who worked there. It was nice and everything, but I tried to explain to the developer that he needed something more.

People were coming in to see the film and look at the exhibits, but they couldn't go into the Mill itself because it was falling apart. I wanted to put a ride in there, maybe a roller coaster, to add to the things they could do, and for them to be able to see what was in the Mill.

The developer thought it would be too expensive and said the film and exhibits were just fine. A few years later, people stopped going to the Mill. I remember talking to the guy, and he said, "You know, for a million dollars, we could have added that ride, and it would have still been going today!" The Mill was abandoned for a long time and then was turned into a restaurant.

CHAPTER 24

RECENT WORK

ven after I retired for good, I still continued to do some work on the side. Nothing big or fancy, just some things to keep me occupied. I've always believed that an artist never stops creating and, trust me, I will continue doing just that until I can't any more. Most of the work I've done after I retired was more for me than anyone else. I explored the things that I enjoyed, and really let myself branch out creatively.

There is this Japanese restaurant in Southern California that I used to love so much. I went there all the time. I started doing some paintings based on it, and eventually donated some of them to the restaurant…in exchange for free food, of course. I also did this beautiful mural for them as well. As far as I know, it's still there today.

I also did a series of paintings of Josephine Baker, who was this amazing African-American singer, dancer, and actress back in the 1930s. Back when I was doing my mobiles at Disney Animation, I had

A piece of my art that once hung in my gallery.
***Opposite:** My recent interpretation of the original sketch Mary Blair did for the It's A Small World façade.*

that book by Alexander Calder. One of the things he had in there was a photo of a wire sculpture of Josephine Baker. I was fascinated by it. Maybe it was the fact that he gave her such enormous breasts made out of corkscrews. That might have had something to do with it. I figured if he did that, she must have been something! Regardless, her name stuck in the back of my head for years.

For years and years, I wondered just who the hell she was. Finally, I went to the library to read up on her. I took out a book written by her son, and I just fell in love with her. I continued to read and learn as much about her as I could. To me, she just seemed so damn sensuous. She did her own thing and didn't give a damn about what other people thought of her. She owned her own nightclub in France, was a wonderful performer and was very exotic. I read once about how she would sometimes go to her club wearing nothing but a fur coat!

Above and opposite: **Paintings of Josephine Baker.**

Anyway, I did a series of paintings of her because she just fascinated me so much. From there, I did a few paintings about the Cotton Club, because she started there back when she lived in America. I have a few of those hanging in my house still.

I also did this series about Day of the Dead. After I retired, I kind of stumbled into this celebration one day in Oceanside. I didn't know anything about it, but all of a sudden, there were these skulls and candles all over the place.

I thought it was a neat subject, so I started looking up information on Day of the Dead. I did a few paintings about it from there. The next year, I went back to Oceanside, and went to a fellow who was working the celebration. I asked him to tell me a little bit more about it, so I could hear about it firsthand. I was even more fascinated.

I told him I'd done some paintings about it, and wondered if he had any space for rent so I could put up a tent and try to sell them, and some of my other work. He directed me toward the guy in charge of the local gallery, who he said might be interested.

I went over to meet the owner of what I was told was called The Phantom Gallery. I told him I wanted to rent a tent nearby to try to sell my paintings in. He told me to come back next week and bring some of my work so he could check it out. So, I went back the next week, portfolio in hand, and after he checked it out, he said "Don't even think about a tent. I want to put this in my gallery as a show!"

I was pretty excited about that. I wound up doing a few shows with him at the gallery. The first one had most

One of my Day of the Dead paintings.

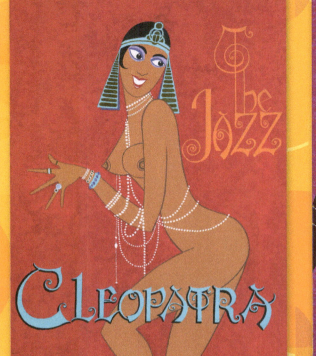

The Jazz

CLEOPATRA

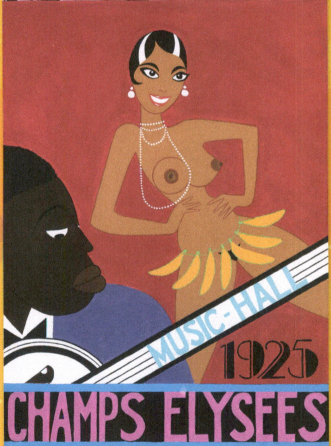

looking like a cross between a baling kangaroo and a piece of chewing gum and a racing cyclist etc.......

Josephine BAKER

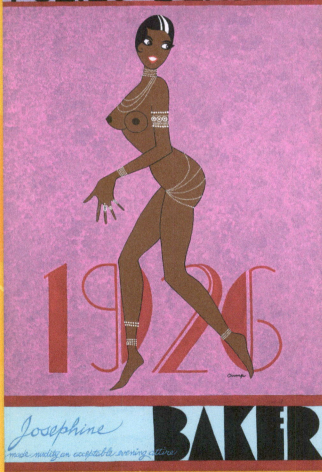

FOLIES BERGERE

1926

Josephine BAKER

made nudity an acceptable evening attire

REVUE NEGRE

MUSIC-HALL 1925

CHAMPS ELYSEES

Some of my Day of the Dead paintings.

of those Japanese and Josephine paintings in it. It went alright, but I didn't sell very many. But that was okay, because a lot of people came, and I got to know most of the locals. More importantly, I also met Marie, the love of my life, on the last day of the gallery show.

The next year during Day of the Dead, though, I put together a great show. I had about 25 Day of the Dead paintings, and I sold damn near every single one of them. I couldn't believe it. I still have a few of those left at home, but most of them are hanging up in houses all over California by now.

I created a line of little bugs recently, too, that I wanted to put on balloons and greeting cards. There is pretty much one for every occasion. A birthday bug (for birthdays), a flu bug (for 'Get Well Soon' cards), a love bug (for Valentine's Day), a humbug (for Christmas) and so on. I did a whole series of them. I wound up with about 24 different bugs. Unfortunately, nothing has come out of them, but there's still hope!

My house is a veritable art museum of my work from throughout my career. Every room has a different theme to it, and represents things that I love. One of the rooms is entirely dedicated to all of my Japanese artwork. Another has my Day of the Dead art. I dabbled in a bit of paper-mache, so I have some of that in my kitchen. Crazy stuff, like lobsters drinking martinis. My bathroom still has those rocks I painted way back in Animation hanging in it! It's almost like walking into a Rolly Crump museum.

A jack-in-the-box, made from paper-mache.

A noblewoman and a jester, made from paper-mache.

Lobster drinking a martini, made from paper-mache, based on a painting I did.

A girl from It's A Small World, made from paper-mache.

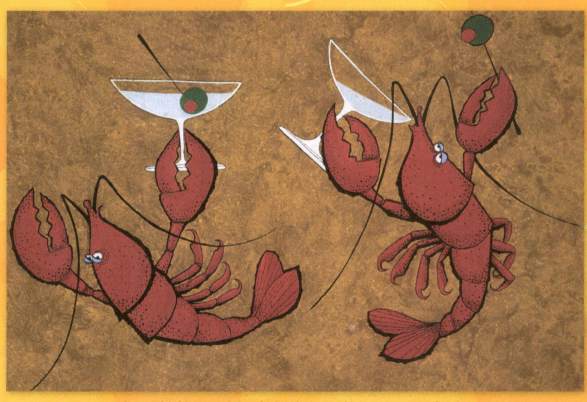

Lobsters drinking martinis, which I also turned into a paper-mache piece.

IT'S KIND OF A CUTE STORY

One of my recent pieces, showing my love of martinis.

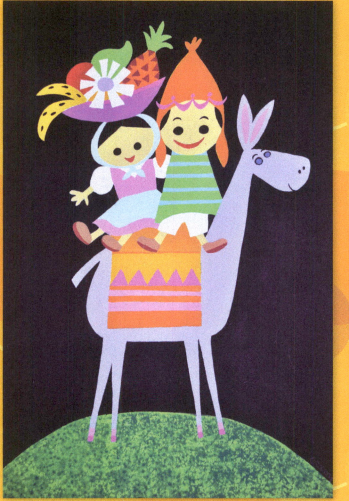

Painting of some children from It's A Small World, based on Mary Blair's style.

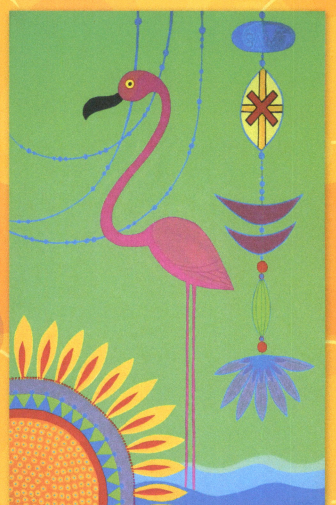

A painting I did for the Yakovetic family.

My take on Adam and Eve, with a door handle placed in an interesting position.

IT'S KIND OF A CUTE STORY

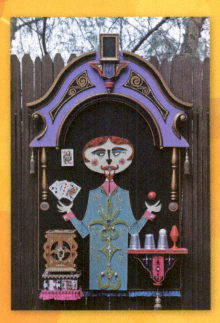

TO JACK MY BEST FOR EVER.
Rolly Crump

Above: A gift from me to a friend.
Top left: A sculpture of a magician that once hung in my backyard.
Middle: A poster in my kitchen.
Bottom: A recent painting I did of Marie.

Discussing the Tower of the Four Winds with Walt after we'd both seen it for the first time at Kelite's construction lot. Signed and personalized by Walt.

WALT

'd like to talk about Walt for a little bit because I loved that man so much. I know he weaves in and out of most of my stories, but I really feel like I wouldn't be where I am today if it wasn't for him.

A lot of people ask me what Walt was like, and there really is no good answer for that. If you ask anyone that knew him personally, you would never get the same answer because he treated everyone differently. Whenever he talked to you, he talked to you on your level. He was genuinely interested in who you were as a person. When you were working at WED, he would ask you about what you were working on, but then start to ask a million questions about your life, your family and other things. He always wanted to know more, especially about the people who worked for him.

When they were getting ready to open up CalArts, the school to help teach artists, I was having a conversation with Walt about possibly teaching there. He shot down that idea because he thought I was going to be too busy on other projects, but while we were on the subject of schooling, he asked me about mine.

"What is your background in art?" he asked me.

"Oh, high school," I replied.

"No, no," he said to me. "I meant in your art."

"I know. I took all the art classes in high school," I told him.

"I mean your professional training," he asked again.

"I went to Chouinard for six Saturdays when I was 16…" He started to laugh at that. He thought I was putting him on.

"How did you learn how to do all this stuff?" he asked.

"Well, honestly," I said, "It's because of you." He was really shocked by that. I wasn't kidding, though. I told him it really was because of him. Like I mentioned earlier, the way he ran the studio was one big open door policy. You could go into any department, and see what they were doing. There were absolutely no barriers.

I could go over to Ink and Paint and watch them mix the paints. I could walk onto a sound stage and watch them set up shots for *20,000 Leagues Under the Sea*. I could watch the background painters do their work. In fact, Eyvind Earle, who did the beautiful backgrounds for *Sleeping Beauty*, taught me how to sponge backgrounds just because I walked into his office one day. I told Walt all of this, and he just smiled.

"I guess that makes you some kind of genius then," he said.

"No, Sir," I replied. "I'm not a genius, you're the genius. Even my mother said how much I've grown since I started here."

He smiled again and said, "I won't argue with your mother then, Rolly. Keep up the good work!"

Walt was delightful to work with because he listened and absorbed what you were saying. He tried to take your idea and bring it to the next level. He'd always be there to support you. He had an unbelievable imagination, and I think that's one of the reasons he and I got along so well. His imagination was always running, and he was always looking for something he had never seen before. Luckily, I think I was able to present him with something he had never seen before almost every time.

Not only that, but he was interested in everyone's opinion on projects, too. Not just the top brass, or the people who worked on them…but everyone. There was this janitor that worked at the Studios named

Claude. He was just one of the sweetest men on the planet. He was sweeping the main corridor of the Animation building one day when Walt walked by. Now, they had just painted that corridor green, so the fresh paint signs were still up and everything.

Walt stopped to have a conversation with Claude, and in the middle of it he asked for his opinion on the new color. He told me later he didn't know what to say, but told him, "Gee, I'm not an artist, but I guess that they're fine." But Walt asked him because Claude was going to be working in that corridor every day, and wanted to make sure he liked it. If he didn't, I have no doubt he would have changed the color to something else.

There is one really great example that shows how much Walt cared what everybody thought about the Park. On the weekends, when he had the time, he would wander around the Park, trailing behind groups of people as they walked around. He dressed down, with his hair messed up a bit, so people wouldn't recognize him. He also had a bad back, so he hunched over out in public, making it even harder for people to identify him. He loved standing in line with the public to find out what they might say about the place. He was tricky like that, but he learned a lot from those little excursions.

He was always interested in what you were doing. He knew he had a lot of weird people working for him, myself included, so he was always receptive to everyone's needs. I remember one time when I was working at Disneyland, I found this beautiful antique gas pump from a gas station that closed years before. It was just sitting there in this big, empty lot, so I had it picked up and sent to WED. I had it outside my office, kind of as a decoration. I thought maybe I would be able to do something with it one day.

It had some gigantic spiders living in it, though, which I hadn't noticed before. Walt came by one day, and saw it out in the hallway.

"Rolly, what's this?" he asked.

"It's an old gas pump," I replied.

"I can see that, but what is it?" he asked.

"I don't know, really. I think I'll do something with it one of these days."

"Oh okay. Well, make sure you kill the spiders first," he said and then walked off. He could have told me to get rid of it, because having those spiders roaming around could have been dangerous. He just left it alone. He didn't question it when he knew you were going to make something great, and I always thanked him for that.

Walt could get cranky, though. He hardly ever did, but when someone deserved it, he certainly got cranky with them. Whenever we knew he was in a mood, word got around the studio fast that "Walt is wearing his bear suit today."

Dick Nunis once said, "When you're playing with Walt, never go for the third strike. You can go after him once, go after him twice…but never go after him three times." Those were true words of wisdom, so I never forgot them.

I remember being in a meeting with Walt and one of the directors of Merchandise at Disneyland. This guy wanted to put t-shirt shops all over Disneyland, but Walt didn't want any part of that. But he kept bringing it up throughout the meeting.

"Walt, we have got to put a t-shirt shop in Bear Country."

"No, I don't like that so much."

"You know, they make a lot of money, Walt."

"We're not going to do that."

That third time he said it, though…Walt let him know for sure it wasn't going to happen. Walt usually never called anybody by anything other than their first name. So he turned to this guy and said, "Mr. Becker, the tail does not wag the dog."

That was the end of that conversation

Walt also had an extremely marvelous sense of humor. It would come out at the strangest times. We would be right in the middle of a meeting, and he'd say, "Oh my God, I'm going to have another granddaughter. I got to tell you about that!"

It didn't matter if the meeting was about something serious or not, he'd just go into these personal stories about his own life, and we'd just go around the table talking. I remember one meeting where he said he'd met his daughter's boyfriend and that she was going to marry him.

"All I can say is I'm going to have beautiful grandchildren," he said, because he was talking about Ron Miller, who was the boyfriend in question and also very, very handsome.

Like I said, Walt had a great imagination, and that's why he called us his Imagineers. He just came up with these wonderful things. That's why he was so successful when he first started out. He used his imagination to tell a great story in the cartoons, and then in films, and then eventually in the Parks.

He really had you go through the gauntlet of emotions with his work. He made you cry, he made you laugh, and he scared the pants off you. He did that in his films, and he continued to do that with the rides at Disneyland. He covered all the bases.

I think the one thing that Walt taught me more about than anything else was the big picture. He had a vision, he knew exactly what it was going to be and how he was going to get there. It was almost like he'd slice through it and he knew every ingredient that was there because he lived it himself to create it.

It was interesting to sit in a meeting with him, because a lot of times you thought he wasn't listening. It was like his mind was somewhere else. That wasn't true though, because he was right there with you. It was just that his brain was going a million miles a minute and he was working it all out in his head.

Whenever I was given a project, I would try to visualize how it would look at the end before I did anything else. I looked at it the way he did, and tried to see what he would have wanted. You had to take everything into consideration. Not just your little piece of the project, but every piece of it. Soon, all the pieces would fall into place, and it would become a reality.

For example, when I was working on an attraction, I had to think about where everything was going to go. Not just in my small piece of it, but where the merchandise areas were, where the restrooms were, and all of that.

I was working with Yale Gracey when we had a meeting with Walt, and he gave us some really good advice.

"You have to remember the electricians. You have to remember the Maintenance guys. You have to work around them, because you can't ignore them," he told us. "They're supporting what you are doing, so you have to support them. Listen to them." He was right, and it was probably the best advice he ever gave me. I think that's why a lot of people at other companies at the time failed. They didn't understand what the big picture was, and that hurt them in the end.

Walt was great because he never told you what to do. Instead, once you got started, he just directed you a little bit. He was very sweet about it. If there was something he didn't like, he never said flat out that he didn't. He took a different approach to it.

Like I mentioned in an earlier chapter, Mary Blair made a presentation to him about one of the scenes for It's A Small World when we were moving it to Disneyland, and Walt didn't like it. She covered all the sets with carpet, which was something totally foreign at the time, and he just didn't like the way it looked. When she was finished, he didn't look at her and say, "Jesus Christ, what the hell is this?"

Instead, he said, "Well, that's a good idea, but let's think about it a different way." He was always very polite, and very aware of how to nurture our creative process.

Well, he was polite most of the time. One the things he hated most were yes men. Of course, owning such a large company, he had a fair share of them. There was one story someone told me about when Walt went to breakfast with some of his upper lever guys…each one of them a yes man in their own way. They were always looking for new ways to kiss up to the boss, and this is one of those times when they really shouldn't have.

The first guy orders ham and eggs.

Next, it's Walt's turn. He orders waffles with strawberries on top.

Before the waitress had a chance to write that down, the first guy says to her, "That sounds really good, Walt. You know what? I want to change my order to waffles with strawberries on top."

The second guy puts down his menu and says, "That does sound good. I'll have waffles with strawberries on top as well.

Of course, the third guy, not wanting to be outdone, also orders waffles with strawberries on top.

Walt just got up from his chair and said, "Son of a bitch!" before walking out of the restaurant. I heard that story when I was still in Animation, and I've always remembered it. When I was first hired into WED, I sat in meetings with Walt for a while before I ever spoke up. All I did was study Walt, his body language, and the way he thought.

I also watched how people would answer him. I was amazed that they were pretty much scared of him. Whatever he said, they went along with. No one ever spoke out against him and I could see that sometimes he would get frustrated with that.

So, I was honest with him from then on. Walt liked people that were honest. I was more honest with him than anyone else, and I think he really liked that about me. In fact, it was kind of cute, because whenever we would have a work session with him, I'd sit next to him. If I was confused when the session was over, I'd grab Walt's sleeve as he tried to leave and pull him back down.

"Rolly, what is it that you want?" he'd ask.

"I hate to ask you this, but I lost your train of thought." Sometimes we were in there for a couple of hours, and I would completely forget just what the meeting was about. I was being honest with him, and would ask him if he could run that by me one more time.

He would sit me down and go, "Okay, this is what I have in mind." Sometimes, because I was so honest with him, he would just come back with, "Well, shit, I don't know either!"

We had a very honest relationship with each other, because even though I spoke my mind, I never got out of line with him.

One of Walt's favorite sayings was, "Oh, for Christ's sake!" It was his basic response to whatever irritated him. It was never a problem in private, but every so often he would forget he was in public and let it slip.

I remember filming that *World of Color* television show with him back in the early 1960s where we were talking about the Tower of the Four Winds. We each had our own lines displayed on a monitor in front of us.

He would read his lines, mess up a bit, and let out an "Oh, for Christ's sake!" so loud everyone around him could hear. It was pretty funny.

During that same filming, Walt began his scripted lines and then went off on a tangent. I was trying to pay close attention to what he was saying so I would know what to say when it was my turn to jump in. All of a sudden, he stopped talking and looked to me.

I completely froze. I had no idea what to say. He totally threw me off.

"Oh, Jesus," I said. "Christ."

We both broke out laughing, and he just shook his head a little and smiled. Then he started speaking again, from the top, and this time it went off without a hitch!

It was always interesting to film shows with Walt, because he said whatever he wanted. Sometimes he'd read from the monitor, other times he'd just go off on his own thing. It would be a challenge to keep up with him.

There's another cute little story about one of Walt's other favorite sayings.

Before I met Walt, when I was still in Animation, his nurse, Hazel George, came to find me. She knew that I was doing some crazy paintings on rocks, and said she wanted me to do one for Walt's Christmas present. I told her I'd be happy to help, and asked her what she wanted me to paint on it.

"I want you to paint the word 'shit' on it," she said to me. "It's his favorite cuss word."

There were only two "shit" rocks ever made: the one I painted for Walt's Christmas present and this one that Jeff Heimbuch, co-author of this book, now owns.

I did, and put it in a beautiful little Japanese box for her to give to him. About a week later, I saw Hazel and I asked, "Well, did Walt get his Christmas present?"

"Oh yeah," she said. "He loved it, and I gave you credit for it!" I don't know what happened to the shit rock, because I always forgot to ask him about it, but I knew he loved it.

Walt was an awfully generous person, too. One time, he and Emile Kuri, one of the original designers of Disneyland, were sitting on the City Hall steps first thing in the morning when the Park was opened for the day. Walt looked up and there was a nun walking with a bunch of kids. She was holding on to a rope, which was attached to the first little kid, and then that kid was attached to another kid, and so on down the line. There was a whole stream of these kids attached to each other by ropes. At the end of the line was another nun. Walt watched them walk by before getting up to introduce himself to the nun in charge.

"What is this about?" he asked her, pointing to the kids. She said that they were underprivileged children that they wanted to bring to Disneyland to have a fun day.

"How much did you pay to get in?" She told him whatever the amount was, and he said "Excuse me, I'll be right back." Walt went right up to the main gate, got her money back, and marched right back to her to give it back.

"No underprivileged children are ever going to have to pay to come into Disneyland," he told her. Obviously that isn't true anymore, but that gives you a little insight as to what the Old Man was really like.

Walt was also pretty helpful to other people in the theme park business. In fact, not a lot of people know this, but Walt helped George Millay when he was trying to get SeaWorld off the ground.

Millay went to Disney and told him he wanted to make his own theme park about fish and other sea life, but had no idea what he was doing. He asked Walt for help, and Walt actually assigned maybe two or three guys, and said "Go help George with whatever he wants to do." He didn't have to do that, but he loaned those guys to George to help him get his park off the ground.

Now, granted, part of it may have been that Walt was thinking ahead, and thought that maybe he might want to do a water park like that someday. But he was very gracious, and tried to share his knowledge of how to work a theme park with other people.

I was at Club 33 once, years after Walt passed away, and I saw Roy Disney across the room. I'd never met Roy before, but he came right over to introduce himself.

"Are you Rolly?" he asked me. "It's a pleasure to meet you. My brother used to talk about you all the time." I thought that was really sweet. We had a unique and special friendship. I was glad he was part of my life, and I hope he was glad I was part of his.

The morning that Walt passed away, John Hench was the one who came to tell me the news. He said, "Now we'll realize how much of our work was really done by Walt." I think that was a beautiful statement, and really goes to show you what an effect he had on all of us.

Beyond any doubt, Walt was a genius in every aspect of his life. Those who worked with him would always say that he had a crystal ball in his back pocket. In everything that mattered, he knew the future and made the correct decisions.

No matter the project, Walt clearly saw its common denominator. He recognized the essential skills and talents of the people he assigned to work on his projects. He always picked the right people. He never talked down to you. He always spoke your language, and he always kept your interests in mind. It amazed me how he could talk to anyone about anything, without skipping a beat, and with perfect sincerity.

Once he chose you for a project, and once he knew you understood that project, he backed you to the hilt, no matter what others said.

I never felt self-conscious talking to Walt. No one did. He had a childlike side, a broad streak of kindness that made you feel welcome in his presence, and that accounted in large part for his success. He seemed to understand everyone, and so his ideas touched everyone.

Walt was able to reach inside you and bring a part of you to the surface that you didn't even know existed. He brought out the best in the people around him.

He brought out the best in me.

CHAPTER 26

LIFE REFLECTIONS

ooking back at all the things I've done and the projects I've worked on, I can't even believe it all myself. It's been great, though. I'm shocked at everything I've done, but I couldn't be happier about it. I look back at photos of myself from when I was 8 months old, 10 years old, 20 years old, 30 years old and so on, and I think to myself, "I've really come a long way."

The bulk of work I've done is really huge, and it's only because I moved around a lot and worked with many different people.

People always ask me what my favorite project was, and my answer is always the same. All of them… including the trash cans. I loved every one of my projects, no matter how big or small.

The thing I love most is a challenge: to be asked to do something that I've never done before. That's about as exciting as it can get because, believe it or not, that's where imagination kicks in. As soon as your imagination kicks in, you're on your way. My entire life has been like that.

There is this great little analogy that I use about broadcasting and receiving. Some people broadcast but they don't receive. Some people receive and don't broadcast. I think the bottom line is knowing how much to broadcast and how much to receive. You have to do both to be able to accomplish wonderful things. I like to believe I found the balance for that.

I've always considered myself lucky that I got to do the things I loved to do. Even when I got to my dream job, working in Disney Animation, I knew that wasn't going to be the end for me. Somebody asked me once, while I was there, what I was going to do after that. My answer was "I really don't know, but I will when the time comes."

I also had a strong belief that everything was going to fall into place. I think that came from my Mom. She'd always say, "Rolly, everything is going to be alright. Look ahead, keep positive and you'll be fine."

I've always been a happy person. I've never really been sad. I accepted everything that came my way, no matter what. I think that's what people should do; accept life as it's handed to them and just enjoy it. Another thing is a sense of humor. You've got to have a sense of humor. If you don't, that's something you've got to work on.

I've been thankful that I've been awarded both the Disney Legend Award and a window on Main Street. Both were wonderful moments in my life.

I remember when I opened the letter that said I was going to get a Disney Legend Award. I couldn't believe it. They were going to make me a Legend? I said there was no way I was going to go to the ceremony. Do you know why?

It was only recently that I finally admitted it to myself, but I didn't think I deserved it. I really didn't. There were so many people that worked for Disney who made it the wonderful place that it is, and I really thought any of them should be getting it instead of me.

Finally, my son said he was going to wrap me up in chains, throw me in the back of a truck, and force me to go! So I went, and it was one of the best moments of my life.

Being named a Disney Legend was great, but getting a window on Main Street was far greater. I was happy about both, but I was so much more excited for the window. To get a window on Main Street, U.S.A.

Opposite: In the backyard of my farm, standing near a gypsy cart I designed.

My Disney Room.

at Disneyland is absolutely one of the greatest things that could possibly happen to an employee of Disney.

The day they revealed it was one of the proudest moments of my life. They had a whole ceremony unveiling two new windows; one for me and one for Don Edgren, who had passed away a few years before. Throughout the event, there was a phone next to the podium that kept ringing. It was always Don, making long-distance calls from Heaven. The Mayor of Main Street relayed the message that Walt was up there, too, and he wanted to know if I could re-design the Pearly Gates.

Not missing a beat, I replied, "How soon does he want it?" much to the delight of the crowd. Thankfully, Walt said there was no rush.

The window shows some of my designs from the Enchanted Tiki Room, the Museum of the Weird and the Tower of the Four Winds. The inscription reads:

> *Fargo's Palm Parlor,*
> *Predictions That Will Haunt You,*
> *Bazaar, Whimsical & Weird,*
> *Designs to Die For,*
> *Roland F. Crump,*
> *Assistant to the Palm Reader*

My window is special to me, not only because it honors me, but because it's hanging in a special place. The building it's on is the only building on Main Street that has a porch. The main design of the window, a hand clutching a flower, is replicated on a smaller sign hanging off the porch as well.

A duplicate of my window on Main Street.

IT'S KIND OF A CUTE STORY

In the backyard of my farm, enjoying a glass of wine near a gypsy cart I designed.

The building is now the China Closet, but it once housed the most infamous shop in all of Disneyland's history. When the Park first opened, a lot of the storefronts were actually stores that were operated by outside vendors. That building is where Hollywood-Maxwell's Intimate Apparel was. In case the name doesn't give it away, it sold bras and underwear. They even had a little mechanical show starring the Wonderful Wizard of Bras. Not exactly the type of place you'd expect to find at Disney, right? It only lasted 6 months before Disney asked them to leave.

It was the oddest shop that was ever on Main Street which, I suppose, suits me pretty well, doesn't it?

It always amazes me when I meet fans of my work. For us, Disneyland was just a job that we had to do. We had no idea it would grow into what it is today. I didn't have a clue that it would still be this amazing place that families gathered in all these years later. I'm also amazed at the types of people that Disney attracts. They have the most interesting and varied groups of fans I have ever met. I was at an event one time and this big guy who was dressed like a Hell's Angel, with long hair, a leather jacket and tattoos everywhere, came over to me. He just melted right in front of me and told me how much he loved my work. People sometimes look at me like I'm a star, but I always remind them that I'm just a regular guy that got lucky.

I feel it's important to pass these stories on because they are all great experiences that I was lucky enough to be a part of. I've led an interesting life and loved every minute of it. I'm just happy that people want to listen.

It's also because I love Walt so much. I feel that all these behind-the-scenes stories about Walt are so precious that I want the public to get a better idea of what the Old Man was really like.

Thank you for taking the time to read about the crazy life I've had. I hope you've enjoyed reading about it as much as I've enjoyed living it.

So, what comes next for me? Well, that's kind of a cute story, too.

But we'll save that for another time.

Rolly Crump

Jeff Heimbuch and Rolly Crump.

CHAPTER 27

AFTERWORD

BY JEFF HEIMBUCH

 can undoubtedly tell you, all bias aside, that Rolly Crump has always been my favorite Imagineer.

My first trip to Walt Disney World was when I was 4 years old. Sure, my memory may be a little fuzzy about the finer points of it now, but thankfully there was an old VHS camera to capture some of the moments that have been burned forever into my memory.

I may have been young, but Disney left a lasting impression on me. I mean, here I am, almost 25 years later, and still writing about it a few times a week!

As I started to get older, I began to wonder more about it. Who built this magical place? How did they do it? Why did they do it?

As the years went on, and I started to amass my Disney knowledge, I found that I was always drawn to very certain and specific things in the Parks: the arms holding the candelabras in the Haunted Mansion; the Tikis with glints in their eyes while they beat the drums in the Enchanted Tiki Room; the wonderful toys of It's A Small World.

While I was fascinated with everything about Disney, these were the things that stuck out in my mind. I had to know more about them.

Little did I know that one man was behind all of them.

I actually first learned of the Imagineers because of my quest to learn more about these seemingly minute details. Now, you have to remember, this was before the online Disney community was as vast as it is today. In fact, there WAS no online Disney community yet, because there was no online yet! Information was a little harder to come by. But, through some old-fashioned research in my local library, I was able to discover this wonderful world *behind* the curtain of magic, and coincidently, Rolly Crump was the first name I came across.

Of course, I knew who Walt Disney was, and he absolutely is considered the original Imagineer. But Rolly was the first one I learned about beyond him. I remember checking out a VHS tape of an episode of *Walt Disney's Wonderful World of Color* from the library, and rushing home to watch it. I'm quite certain that this wasn't an 'official' VHS release, but rather a homegrown copy, now that I think about it. But regardless, I popped it in, and was entranced by the glimpses of WED that it showed.

And then came the crowning moment; Walt took the girl he was showing around to a corner of the room to look at all these weird models. The man he asked to help explain them? Why, it was none other than Rolly Crump, of course.

After that, I became obsessed. I read up on everything that helped create the magic of Disney. The wonderful world of WED came alive in my mind and took on a legendary status. Soon, I started to learn the names of all the other Imagineering greats but, somehow, everything I read always came back to Rolly. He was always associated with stuff that was a little off-the-wall and outside the norm. He sounded like the type of guy I wouldn't mind hanging out with!

Flash forward to years later, when I first started writing about Disney seriously. I was writing my *From the Mouth of the Mouse* column, where I would interview past and present Cast Members. Up until that point, I had only spoken with people on the front lines, learning more about their day to day responsibilities.

Rolly had just released his 45 minute audio tour of Disneyland, *A Walk in the Park*, and I thought 'What the hell, let me email him to see if he would be interested in talking to some kid from Jersey who grew up admiring his work.'

Thankfully, he was all for it.

So, one Saturday afternoon, I set up a mini recording studio in my fiancée's closet and called Rolly Crump.

I won't lie to you; talking to a man I've looked up to and admired for years was nerve-wracking. But I found that, while speaking with him, he was an absolute delight. What was supposed to be a 20 minute interview turned into an almost 2 hour conversation between myself, Rolly and Marie.

He was quite possibly the most laidback and hilarious person I had ever spoken with. Despite my telling him what an honor it was to speak with him, he had to keep reminding me that he was "...just a regular guy that got lucky."

After the interview was over, I was thrilled. I could have been happy with just that. But, as luck would have it, I wasn't through with Mr. Crump just yet.

A few months later, Rolly began writing a short, weekly column for the same site as me, detailing some of his adventures at Disney. I looked forward to reading his exploits every week because they were always so crazy.

'Someone should really help this guy turn this into a book,' I kept thinking.

It wasn't long after that I was invited to be that someone.

I was absolutely floored! How the hell did I get to be so lucky?

Of course, I accepted. How could I not? A chance to work side by side with my favorite Imagineer of all time? Absolutely! It was a once in a lifetime opportunity, and I dove in head first.

I flew across the country shortly after that to spend some time with Rolly and to start working on the book. During that time, I was able to go through his personal archives of everything he ever worked on (and let me tell you, this stuff can probably rival the Disney Archives!). His house was like a living museum of Disney and theme park history. It was a truly incredible experience.

So, over the course of the last year, armed with photos documenting Rolly's life, theme park history notes and over 100 hours of audio interviews I conducted with the man himself, I set out to craft his story into what you now hold in your hands.

It was a daunting task, but it was a labor of love.

I really hope you enjoyed reading Rolly's life story as much as we enjoyed putting it together. There aren't a lot of folks left these days with firsthand accounts of working at the Studio, at WED, or even directly with Walt, so I'm glad that Rolly shared his story with not only me, but with all of you as well. It's important from a history aspect that theme park enthusiasts know this stuff, not only because they are important from a Disney standpoint, but also because they are fantastic stories as well.

Rolly is such a great storyteller that it makes it so much easier to enjoy these stories. He's not lecturing you about the ins and outs of the business. He's sitting you down, pouring you a few drinks, and just letting it all come out (which, quite honestly, is exactly how we spent most of the nights I spent out in California working with him).

The guy who I grew up admiring and loving his work now calls me his "adopted grandson."

Surreal? Absolutely. Hard work? Totally. Worth every minute? Without a doubt. I still have to pinch myself every so often to make sure this hasn't all been a dream.

Not only is Rolly a truly gifted artist and an incredibly creative mind, but he is one of the sweetest, most genuine people I have ever met in my entire life. He helped shape the direction my life was going in well before I ever met him, and continues to do so to this day. But most important of all, he's my friend. And that, ladies and gentlemen, made it all well worth it for me.

IT'S KIND OF A CUTE STORY

ROLAND F. CRUMP

Executive Designer • WALT DISNEY IMAGINEERING • 1992 to 1996

Rejoined The Walt Disney Company and was assigned to be Supervising Art Director for EPCOT. Responsibilities included:

→ Re-design parts of The Land pavilion including a new interior for the Great Hall.
→ Replace the Kitchen Kabaret attraction with Food Rocks. The total budget for the refurbishing of the pavilion was $20 million.
→ Re-design CommuniCore as the art director and co-designer of various displays and shows. This attraction is a permanent trade show called Innoventions with multiple sponsors and displays of leading edge home, automobile, and personal products for the consumer.

Vice President of Creative • RIDE & SHOW ENGINEERING • 1990 to 1992

Worked on total concepts for theme parks and attractions. Fieldwork locations: Japan, Korea, Turkey, Germany, and Africa.

Art Direction Consultant • MECCA • 1989 to 1990

Art Direction for dinner show restaurant and stand-alone attractions. Directed concept design for the Communication pavilion built for the 1993 Taedon EXPO in Seoul, Korea.

Art Direction Consultant • CINEMATIX • 1998 to 1989

Development of major entertainment attractions for Mitsubishi company to be located throughout Tokyo, Japan.

President • MARIPOSA DESIGN GROUP • 1986 to 1987

Clients included:

→ Sidney Shlenker, to design and supervise the manufacturing process for four restaurants for the McNichols Sports Arena in Denver, Colorado. Included in the restaurant designs were three animated shows.
→ Stardust Hotel in Las Vegas Nevada, to design the Gambling Hall of Fame, which included the largest collection of antique slot machines in the world.
→ Jacques Cousteau, to act as Art Director for the Cousteau Center in Paris, France which was under construction.
→ A theme park I designed the master plan for in Melbourne, Australia.

President and Sole Owner • MARIPOSA GROUP • 1984 to 1986

Bought out the Mariposa Group from Warner Communications and renamed company to Mariposa Design Group.

→ Designed and manufactured, with the aid of AVG, the Real Time Maze Shootout. This maze is now in operation in the Edmonton Mall in Alberta, Canada and The Sherman Oaks Galleria in California.

→ Designed and manufactured, with the aid of AVG, 40 monuments for Oman for an international celebration.

→ Designed a theme park for Portugal based on the years of discovery during 1400 to 1500.

Creative Director • MARIPOSA GROUP • 1983 to 1984

Projects included:

→ The master plan for the rehabilitation of Fair Park in Dallas, Texas.

→ An animated show for the Sultan of Oman located in a Portuguese fort that was built in 1400.

→ Designs for the Cousteau Ocean Center in Paris, France and Cousteau Ocean Center in St. Louis, Missouri.

Project Lead • THE COUSTEAU SOCIETY • 1982 to 1983

Headed up a design team to design the Cousteau Ocean Center. This was a $30 million project scheduled to be built in Norfolk, Virginia. The Cousteau Society administration then concluded that more than one facility should be built and studies were done to find other sites around the world for this project.

Director of Special Projects • ATLANDIA DESIGN & FURNISHINGS • 1981 to 1982

Designed and produced an animated bird show for the Golden Nugget Hotel's lobby in Atlantic City, New Jersey. The show was performed in a 50 foot high solid brass bird cage and cycled every 15 minutes. The cost of this show was $500,000 and was the most sophisticated show of its size in the world at the time of completion.

Art Director • WED ENTERPRISES • 1977 to 1981

Rejoined WED full-time as a Project Designer on the new billion-dollar EPCOT. Project was built in Florida and opened in October 1982. Responsibilities included designing two of the major pavilions, Life and Health and The Land, and also participated in the marketing these concepts to the American industry for a joint venture with Disney. The Land pavilion was sponsored by Kraft Corporation and the estimated cost was $88 million. Other responsibilities included working in conjunction with Disneyland Park on a 15 year expansion master plan.

Consultant Designer • WED ENTERPRISES • 1976 to 1977

Consulted with WED as an art director and in charge of a $45 million expansion of Disneyland.

Master Planner • KAHE POINT • 1976 to 1977

Contracted by the Green Brothers to master plan and design a 20 acre theme park using the Islands of the Pacific as a theme. After master planning and giving presentations to the mayor of Honolulu and the governor of the state, a land use permit was to be issued. This project was then turned over to Bill Martina due to my contract with WED.

Art Director • GOLDEN NUGGET • 1976 to 1977

Contracted by Steve Wynn to re-design the logo of the gambling hall and to see that all signage, graphics and advertising worked well with the theme of the club. Also helped in the execution of the new $20 million Golden Nugget Hotel, which opened in 1977.

Art Director • WELCH FOODS • 1976 to 1977

Contracted to design a hospitality house for the corporation to be used to illustrate to the public the history of the Welch company. The project was put on hold due to lack of funding. A Welch Fun Factory was designed and manufactured and is now being held by Welch pending a new location.

Consultant Designer • KAHUKU SUGAR MILL • 1975

Designed a museum and theater for the old Kahuku Sugar Mill on the island of Oahu. The Sugar Mill was developed by the Liljenwall Group and the Blackfield Corporation into a shopping complex and paid attraction, presenting the history of the sugar industry in Hawaii.

Consultant Designer • SEVEN SEAS • 1975

Contracted to design and complete a cosmetic program for a $17 million theme park for this joint venture between Leisure Marine of San Diego and American Broadcasting Company. Responsibilities included color keying of all structures, decorating of food and merchandise locations and the total design of all signage and graphics associated with the project.

Consultant Designer • SILVER SPRINGS • 1975

Contracted by American Broadcasting Company to work in concert with Ron McMahon and Associates (Architects) to develop a themed entrance complex for Silver Springs Park.

Designer • ABC WILDLIFE PRESERVE • 1974 to 1975

Contracted by American Broadcasting Company to develop a thematic concept for the $17 million Wildlife Preserve. This program resulted in selecting a theme and then administrating the concept from design through installation. All structures were themed inclusive of exterior roof and wall treatments employing techniques ranging from wall graphics and murals to thatched roofs. Signs and graphics, props and dressings and character costumes were part of the theming program. All production items such as tikis, banners and assorted props and dressings were personally produced or production was coordinated per the agreement. Working with Ron McMahon and Associates, the project was completed for the budgeted amount of $3 million.

Master Planner • FABULAND • 1974

Contracted by the Fabuland Corporation to design and master plan a theme park for Paris, France. Completed the master plan, then spent time in Paris with the Fabuland staff preparing the project. The project was abandoned due to France going into a recession.

Consultant Art Director • WET 'N WILD • 1974

Consulted to George Millay of Leisure Marine which developed a new concept in outdoor entertainment. Primary responsibilities were to art direct in thematic and architectural continuity. Specific programs included site plans, rendering, design and presentation models.

Designer • KNOTT'S BERRY FARM • 1974 to 1975

Contracted by Marion Knott to design and install a themed dark ride, Knott's Bear-y Tales. This attraction employed concepts never before applied in a dark ride. Responsibilities were defined as developing the attraction from a design standpoint, then administering all design and production teams in order to open on schedule and within budget. In less than one year the attraction opened for the budgeted $2 million and had achieved the reputation of being highly innovative, yet practical, from an operational perspective.

Director of Design • CIRCUS WORLD • 1973 to 1974

Developed an in-house design team of architects, artists and graphics specialists to assume the overall design responsibilities of the $80 million, 600 acre Circus World project. All aspects of design, land use plan, show concept development, signage and graphics, themed merchandise, costumes, etc. were the responsibility of the design team.

      The project was master planned with study and presentation models and a Preview Center was designed and opened in less than a year. The Center was a unique structure housing food, merchandise and restroom functions with a preshow and a 600 seat theater. The Center cost $4 million and opened as scheduled.

President • DESIGN 27 • 1970 to 1973

Founded a design group and engaged in a diversity of themed architectural design projects for various land development companies across the nation. Clients included:

→ FRANK LA COKE, DEVELOPER – Land development group. Formulated the master plan for a $7 million themed shopping center on 5 acres in Dallas, Texas. Responsibilities included conceptual design of all exteriors, inclusive of landscaping, for two-story, 218,030 square foot structure containing approximately 25 merchandising outlets and four major restaurants and lounges on the ground floor with professional offices above.

→ DEANE & DEAN DEVELOPERS – Large land development group. Responsible for all design aspects of a fishing-village themed commercial area at Half Moon Bay just south of San Francisco, California. Project involved the formulation of master land usage plan and responsibility for all design aspects of landscaping, exteriors, and interiors of this planned oceanside, commercial area which included themed merchandising outlets, restaurants and lounges. Project placed on hold pending resolution of environmental issues.

→ ANHEUSER-BUSCH – Contracted to develop a $500,000 themed black light attraction for the company's Busch Gardens facility in Tampa, Florida. Responsibilities included the development of a theme and the design of all show aspects of the attraction including illusions, fighting, props and dressings and associated exteriors. Also designed a 5 year master plan for the Busch Gardens in Los Angeles.

→ ASTROWORLD – Developed the County Fair area of the AstroWorld. Park. Responsibilities included the design of themed attractions, merchandising outlets and food and beverage facilities. The area was opened to the public in 1972 at a total cost of over $4 million. Also designed all walkaround characters including "Marvel McFey." Design 27 was an art director service for AstroWorld for over two years.

Responsibilities for designing and engendering subsidiary of Walt Disney Productions were many and varied:

→ WALT DISNEY WORLD – Functioned as a Project Designer on the development of a number of major attractions for Walt Disney World during the period from 1969 to 1970. Small World was again re-designed. Also re-designed Mr. Toad's Wild Ride and increased its size to twice that of the attraction at Disneyland. Designed the interior of the Magic Shop on Main Street.

→ DISNEY ON PARADE – Responsibilities for this NBC Television / Walt Disney Productions joint venture included development of story content and design of all sets, props and dressings for the 1970 show season.

→ DISNEYLAND – Served as Supervising Art Director for Disneyland for the period from 1967 to 1969. Primary responsibility was to serve as design representative for all new construction and facilities rehabilitation which occurred in the Park. Scope of activities covered exteriors, interiors, show design, props, dressings, etc. for all areas and facilities within the Park.

→ TOMORROWLAND – One of several Project Designers responsible for the extensive rehabilitation of this area of Disneyland during 1966; activities included the design of the elevator and Tomorrowland Bandstands, Character Corner merchandising facility, ticket booths and the area's numerous themed sculpture pieces.

→ IT'S A SMALL WORLD – Much of 1965 was occupied as Project Designer for the re-design and rehabilitation of the attraction in preparation for its 1966 relocation to Disneyland from the World's Fair site. Activities included the re-design of all interiors and exterior facades and the addition of the Small World clock.

→ HAUNTED MANSION – Worked again on this project over the period of 1964 to 1965 and for a short time in 1966. During these intervals the concept of the show was finalized and the technical aspects of the illusions were developed in preparation for the opening in 1967.

→ WORLD'S FAIR – Beginning in early 1962, worked as a co-designer developing the Ford pavilion for Ford Motor Company at the 1964 World's Fair in New York City. Contract called for the total design of the $25 million facility including theme development and the design of all show aspects of the primeval world display and associated interiors and exteriors. During this same period, I was involved in the conceptualization and design of Pepsi-Cola's Small World Exhibition at the World's Fair. Responsibilities included design of the Tower of the Four Winds and of all toys, props and dressings utilized in the original multi-million dollar facility.

→ ENCHANTED TIKI ROOM AND ADVENTURELAND BAZAAR – Over the period of 1961 to 1963, functioned as Project Designer on the development and design of the Tiki Room attraction and Adventureland Bazaar merchandising area which were installed at Disneyland in 1963 at a total cost of several million dollars. Responsible for the preshow design aspects of the projects including the development and design of the show, props, dressings and interiors and exteriors of the facilities.

→ HAUNTED MANSION – Over the period of 1959 to 1961, functioned as co-designer for the initial conceptualization of the Haunted Mansion attraction ultimately installed at Disneyland and Walt Disney World. Developed total conceptual design including the formulation of over 100 illusions and the construction of numerous full scale incremental models of the attraction.

Assistant Animator • WALT DISNEY PRODUCTIONS • 1952 to 1959

Started with the Disney organization in 1952 as an inbetweener on the animated feature *Peter Pan*. From there, worked up to assistant animator on the features *Lady and the Tramp*, *Sleeping Beauty* and *101 Dalmatians*.

ABOUT THE AUTHORS

ROLLY CRUMP

Born February 27th, 1930, in Alhambra, California, Rolly took a pay cut as a dipper in a ceramic factory to work for Walt Disney in 1952, and, to help pay bills, made sewer manholes on weekends. He served as an inbetweener, and later as an assistant animator, on various classic Disney films.

In 1959, he joined WED, now known as Walt Disney Imagineering. There, he became one of Walt's key designers for some of Disneyland's groundbreaking new attractions and shops, including the Haunted Mansion, the Enchanted Tiki Room, It's A Small World and Adventureland Bazaar. He continued working on and off for Disney for years, including consulting for projects such as Walt Disney World's Magic Kingdom and EPCOT.

Aside from Disney, Rolly consulted on projects including the ABC Wildlife Preserve, Circus World, the Cousteau Ocean Center, and much more.

JEFF HEIMBUCH

Since the first time he stepped foot in the Magic Kingdom at the age of 4, Jeff couldn't get enough. When he was old enough to finally understand how the magic happened, he fell in love even more. For years, Jeff has written on the various topics of Disney for a variety of publications, including several fansites and magazines. Jeff also co-hosts the popular theme park history podcast *Communicore Weekly*. Visit www.jeffheimbuch.com to see what he's up to.

News, events, book signings and more photos can be found at www.itskindofacutestory.com